# HomeMade

# HomeMade

## 101 EASY- TO-MAKE THINGS FOR YOUR GARDEN, HOME, OR FARM

By Ken Braren
& Roger Griffith

GARDEN WAY  PUBLISHING
Charlotte, VT 05445

*Designed, with cover, by Trezzo/Braren Studio*

*Printed in the United States by Capital City Press*

*Fifth Printing, July 1981*

*Illustrations by Ken Braren*

**Library of Congress Cataloging in Publication Data**

Braren, Ken, 1934–
☐ Homemade: 101 easy-to-make things for your garden,
house, or farm.

☐ 1.  Building.  2.  Do-it-yourself work.  I.  Griffith,
Roger, 1919–    joint author.  II.  Title.
TH153.B65        690'.8          77-2887
ISBN  0–88266–103–5

# Part 1

## EASY-TO-MAKE THINGS FOR YOUR HOME

## Contents

# Part 2

## EASY~ TO~MAKE THINGS FOR YOUR GARDEN

## Contents

# Part 3

# EASY-TO-MAKE THINGS FOR YOUR FARM

## Contents

# Dedication

To anyone with a green thumb
who has ever held a hammer.

# Introduction

This is a book about saving, written to help you save money, resources, and that most precious of all of your possessions, time.

It will be a success if, as you look through it, you stop several times and say, "That's for me. I need it." And then, of course, you build it and find it works just as you hoped it would.

Never should you say, "I'd like that, but I never could build it." Have faith in your own abilities, and test them as well. Most of these projects are simple to build. You don't need the skills and experience of a carpenter, nor his array of power tools. Common sense is helpful, and should steer you as you fit some of these ideas to your own individual needs. As for tools, the basic hand tools are all that are needed.

Perhaps you will study one of these pages, then say to yourself, "I know an even better way of building that." Or, after you look through this book, you may say, "They should have included a . . . ." boxtrap or a children's swing or something else used in the home or garden or on the farm. You may remember some favorite project and wish it could have been included in this book. What do you do if this happens? Write to us here at Garden Way Publishing, Charlotte, VT, 05445, and tell us. In that way you can be a contributor in our next printing of this book.

Only two of us are listed as authors of this book, and that listing is not quite true. Friends, neighbors, relatives, Garden Way authors, all have contributed, in the hopes that these ideas and solutions to problems will be passed along to you, and make your life a little easier or more pleasant. To all of them we owe our thanks.

KEN BRAREN
ROGER GRIFFITH

# Part 1

# EASY-TO-MAKE THINGS FOR YOUR HOME

# Sawhorse

Before you go too far into this book, selecting projects that will simplify life for you, look over the next few pages. There are some suggestions that might make work on those future projects a little easier.

The first one is this sawhorse. There's nothing fancy about it, but it has several good points. And one of them is that the legs are braced in two directions. That makes it a steady sawhorse, guaranteed not to wiggle and twist when you're sawing on it.

For a sturdier model, make the legs of 2"x4"s, and inset them one inch into the 2"x6" top.

Two of these can be handy, as legs for a temporary workbench, or to hold lengthy lumber for sawing.

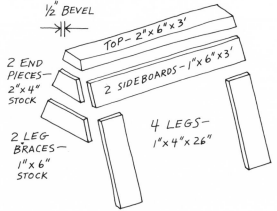

½" BEVEL

TOP — 2"x6"x3'

2 END PIECES — 2"x4" STOCK

2 SIDEBOARDS — 1"x6"x3'

4 LEGS — 1"x4"x26"

2 LEG BRACES — 1"x6" STOCK

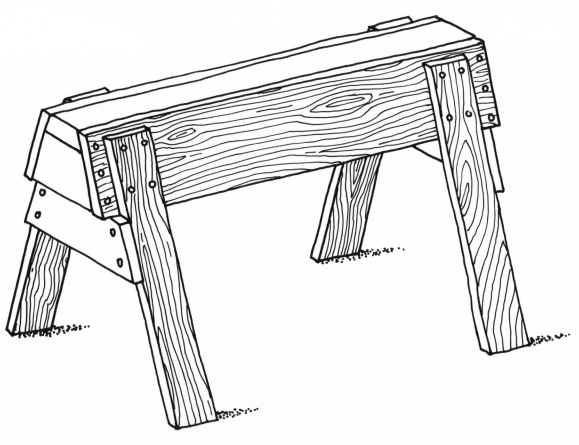

# Carpenter's Tool Box

Scrap one-inch lumber and a sturdy dowel—or a section of a broom handle—and you're ready to build this carpenter's tool box. Load it up in your workshop with the tools you need for that job at the other end of the house, or somewhere outside, and chances are you will save yourself a trip or two back to the shop. Designed by the Extension Service at Michigan State College, this tool box is strong, pleasing in appearance and a good size—a saw will fit in comfortably.

The dowel can be fixed into place by drilling holes through the end pieces, then glueing the dowel in position.

If you're the kind who loses tiny tools such as drill bits, make a compartment or two at one end of this tool box. If the partition for the compartment is no more than three inches high, it will not interfere with the placement of larger tools.

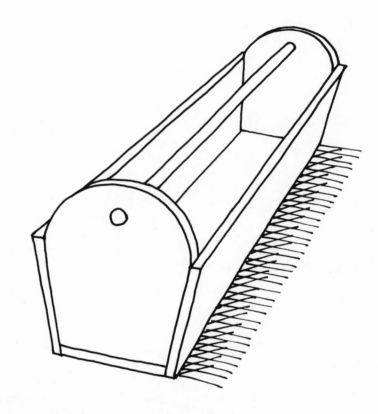

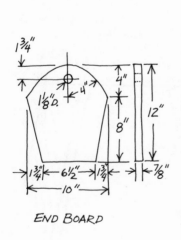

END BOARD

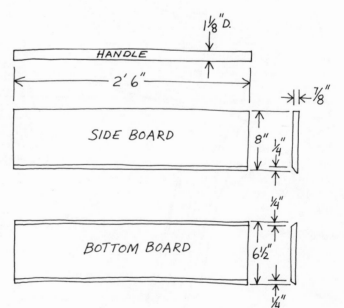

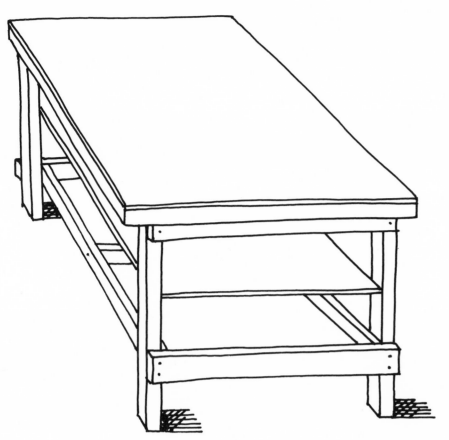

# Workbench

A workbench is a must. It should be big enough to handle a variety of jobs, sturdy enough so that you never think about its strength, and not so fancy that you hesitate to use it for fear you may mar it.

This one fills all of those requirements. It is six feet long, 28½ inches wide, which is a good working size. If you bolt together the 2″x4″ frame, instead of using nails, it will be sturdy. And the Masonite quarter-inch tempered presdwood top and shelf will take a lot of abuse, and can be cut from one 4′x6′ panel.

As you will note in the drawing, all of the lumber required for this is easily obtained, being either 2″x4″ or 2″x10″. Three pieces of 2″x10″ each six feet long, are needed for the top.

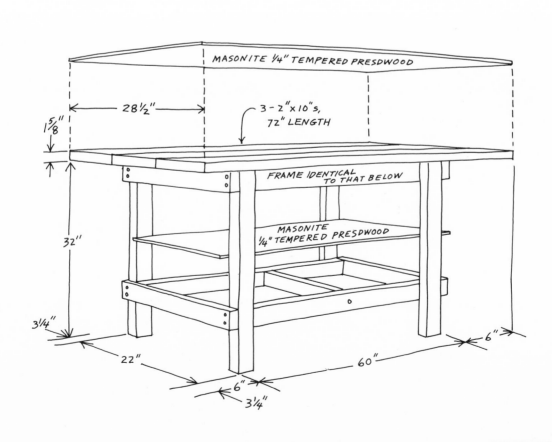

MASONITE ¼″ TEMPERED PRESDWOOD

28½″

1⅝″

3 - 2″x10″s, 72″ LENGTH

FRAME IDENTICAL TO THAT BELOW

MASONITE ¼″ TEMPERED PRESDWOOD

32″

3¼″

22″

6″

3¼″

60″

6″

# Basement Closet

That space under the basement stairs is usually wasted, or is a catchall for unwanted or unmended articles.

A common way to get maximum use from this closet is to install shelving in the rear, leaving the front open for storage of larger things.

Drop a plumb line from the top end of each stringer, and mark the spots on the basement floor as the front corners of the closet. Use 2″x4″s, with the four-inch side down, to outline the base of the closet. Secure them with expansion bolts in the concrete. Uprights, again made of 2″x4″s, are placed from the end of the base to the top of the stringers, with the top of the 2″x4″s cut at an angle to fit to the slant of the stringer. If a door is to be included, its framing should be built now. Also uprights should be placed about midway the length of the closet, again cut at a diagonal on top to fit the slant of the stringer. Careful placement of them will eliminate non-essential cutting of plywood or hardwood sides which will be 4′x8′ sheets. Unless stairs are closed in, a slanting closet back should be fitted in under the stairs. Before closing in closet, nail 2″x4″s between uprights, on either side, and use one-inch tongue-and-groove stock for shelving where it is desired. Installation of a light fixture will dramatically increase the convenience of this big storage space.

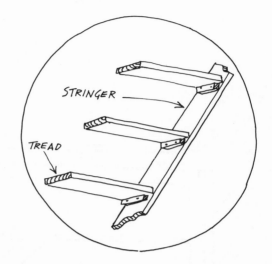

STRINGER

TREAD

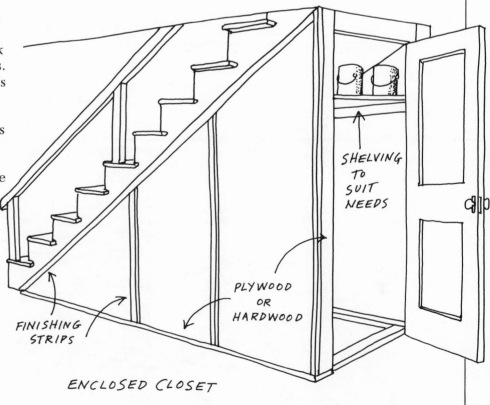

SHELVING TO SUIT NEEDS

PLYWOOD OR HARDWOOD

FINISHING STRIPS

ENCLOSED CLOSET

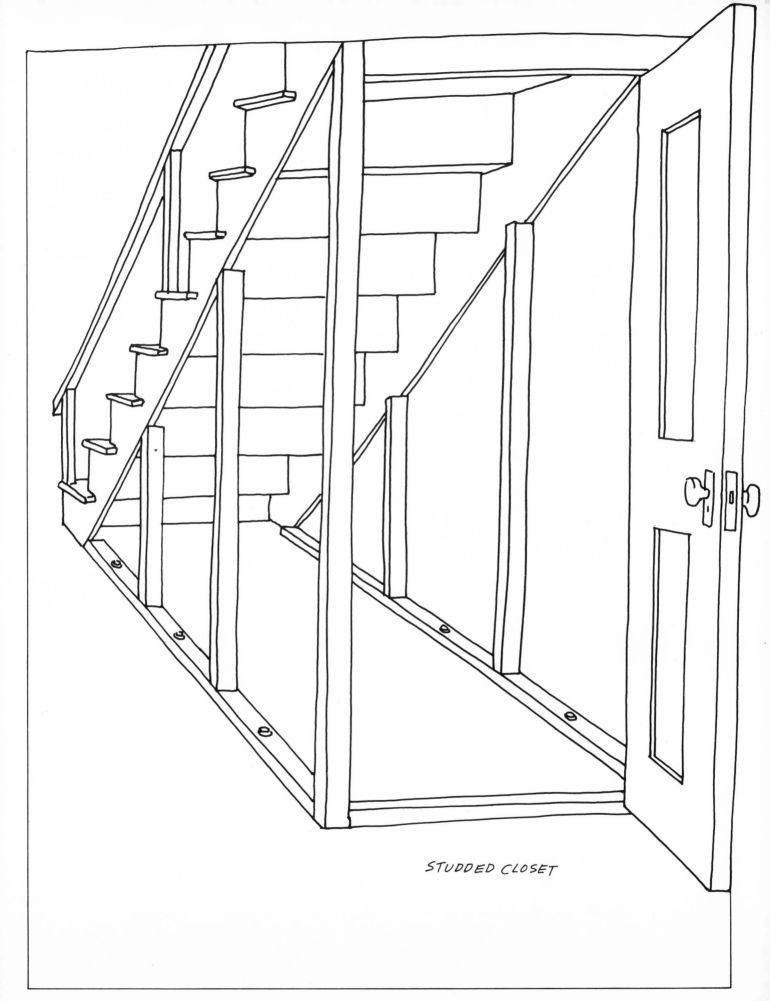

STUDDED CLOSET

# Potting Bench

Whether you are repotting that old begonia or shifting 100 tomato plants from flats to peat pots, a work space is invaluable, and makes the job a pleasure. On this and succeeding pages are suggestions for your garden work center equipment.

A potting bench is a must—and don't have it double for any other purpose or it will be a cluttered nuisance. Here are two models suggested by the California Redwood Association people. One is free-standing. The other can be built to be fastened to the 2″x4″s in your garage or another outbuilding. Build either to the height you prefer (32″-36″ is usually about right) and make it roomy in depth, yet not so wide it is difficult to reach across. Four feet is a convenient length. Make it rugged—two-inch thick material is best. On the free-stand model, a shelf underneath will provide storage space (great for those extra clay pots) and brace the bench as well.

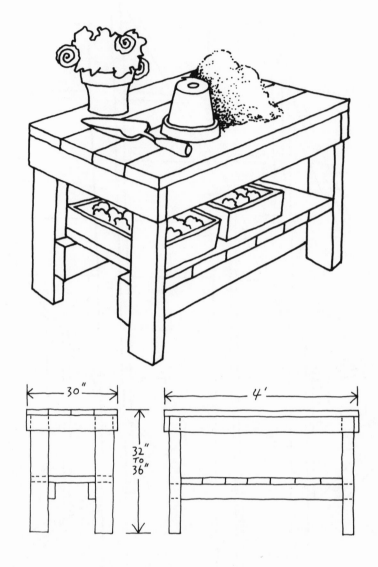

# Sandpaper Block

Ever had a big sandpapering job, and wound up sandpapering your knuckles better than the wood to be sandpapered?

If so, you'll appreciate the suggestion of Bruce Williamson of Charlotte, Vt. Bruce used two pieces of 1x4, about six inches long. He fastened them together with two pieces of an old belt acting as hinges. Then he hammered about six finishing nails through the top piece of 1x4, so that the points came out in the center of this board sandwich. Next he cut a piece of sandpaper that would wrap around the lower block, and the ends could be positioned between the two blocks. He shut the top piece to the lower piece, and the nails held the sandpaper in place while he went to work, knuckles free of sandpapering.

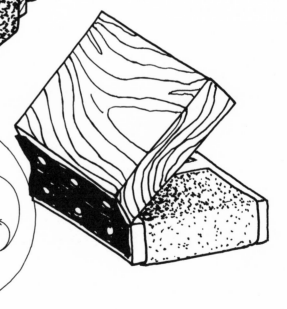

6-1¼"
FINISHING
NAILS

2-1x4 6"LONG
OLD BELT FASTENED
WITH 6-½"NAILS

# Brush Cleaner

Here are two hints that will make your handyperson work a lot easier.

When you look for a paint brush, do you find paint-hardened veterans, or brushes that you left to soak, and now they have bristles that are curled and ruined? You need this little money-saver, so you don't rush out for a new brush for each paint job.

Cut a seven-inch receptacle like the one shown by removing the top section of a gallon varnish can. Notch facing sides. Drill holes in the handles of your brushes, just above the ferrule. Put a round metal rod or piece of heavy wire that won't bend through the holes, and set them in your pan, into which you will put a half-and-half mixture of turpentine and linseed oil. This of course should be used only for brushes used when a painting project is interrupted for a few days.

For storage of brushes, clean them, generally with the material used as a thinner for your paint, then hang them up to dry. To clean out oil paints, varnishes and enamel, use turpentine, then detergent in water; for lacquer, use lacquer thinner or acetone; for shellac use denatured alcohol, then soap and water; for water-type paints, use clear water or water and detergent. Nylon brushes sometimes are more difficult to clean. Work out the paint by using the proper thinner, and brushing on newspapers, then use the thinner to clean the brush. Overnight soaking in the thinner is recommended if cleaning is difficult.

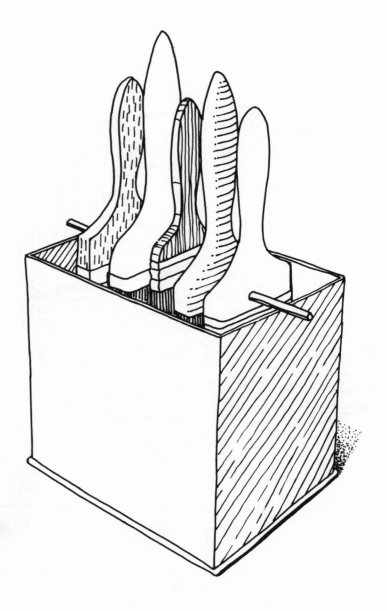

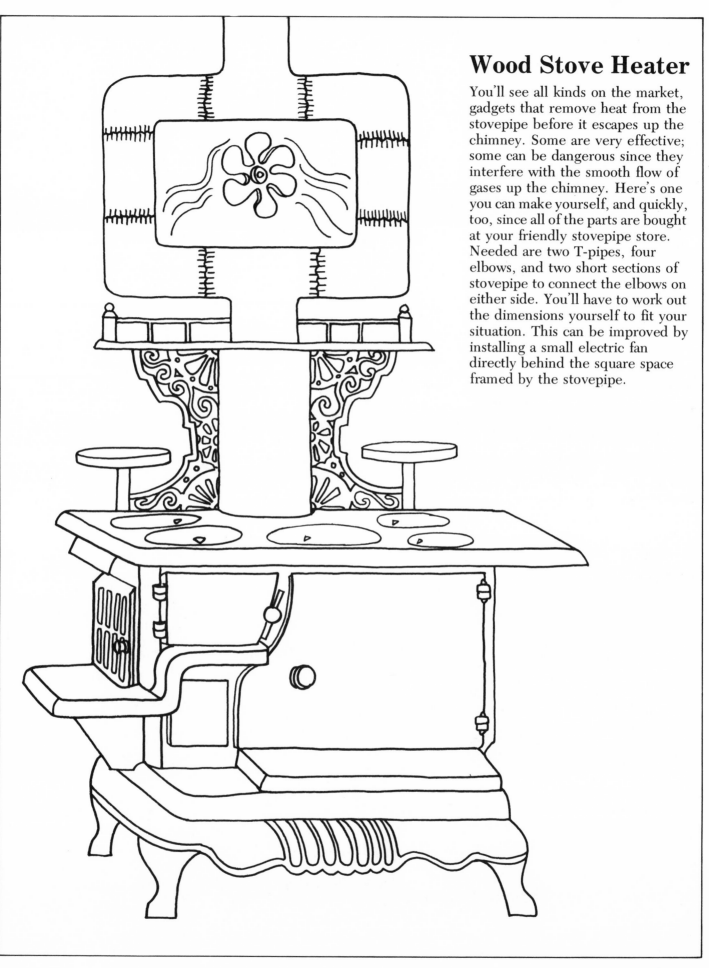

# Wood Stove Heater

You'll see all kinds on the market, gadgets that remove heat from the stovepipe before it escapes up the chimney. Some are very effective; some can be dangerous since they interfere with the smooth flow of gases up the chimney. Here's one you can make yourself, and quickly, too, since all of the parts are bought at your friendly stovepipe store. Needed are two T-pipes, four elbows, and two short sections of stovepipe to connect the elbows on either side. You'll have to work out the dimensions yourself to fit your situation. This can be improved by installing a small electric fan directly behind the square space framed by the stovepipe.

# Firewood Brace

We've all done it. We've carefully piled up firewood, braced at one end by a wall or something equally firm. The pile looked just fine for one day—then someone took a piece of wood from it, and down rolled the wood from the unbraced end. Here's a brace that will let you avoid that. Our homesteader in Hudson, Maine, who suggested this said to use a rugged 2″x6″ board, sawing to provide a 36″ upright and an 18″ base. Nail them together, but get the strength from the diagonal support. He used a piece of 1″x3″, and attached it with heavy wood screws that would support the weight. He uses this on his back porch.

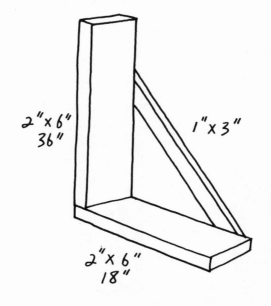

2″x6″
36″

1″x3″

2″x6″
18″

WALL

BRACE

# Sawbuck

If you want a dull chainsaw and a sore back, cut up logs while they are lying on the ground. This sawbuck, pictured in Larry Gay's *Heating with Wood*, can be made in only a few minutes and will save you hours of effort and headache. Use sturdy materials, 2″x8″ is good, and link the two ends with two cross pieces. It will last a lifetime of hard work if bolted together securely.

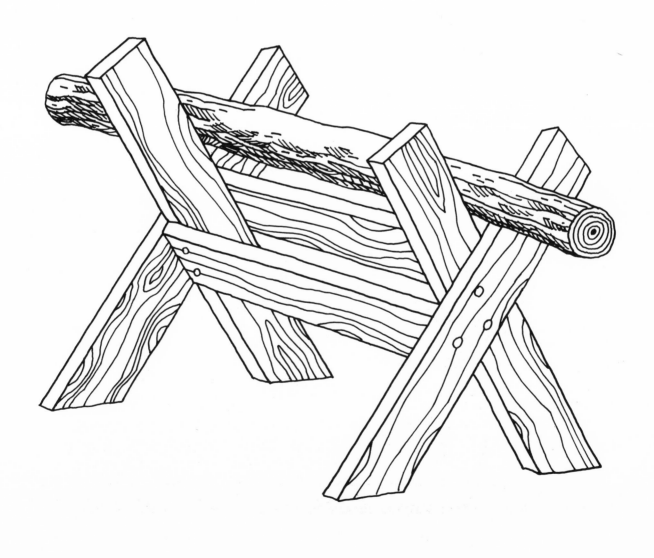

# Fuel Sled

Here are some projects for the family that is saving money and fossil fuel by using wood for heating.

If you're moving small logs before cutting them, a sled of some kind is a must. A children's sled is too small and fragile for much of a load; a toboggan won't carry very much.

This sled (see illustration) was designed and built by Rockwell Stephens, author of *One Man's Forest*. The runners are old hickory skis (cheap at any auction), cut down to four feet in length. A three-foot block of sturdy hardwood, at least 2″x8″, is fastened to each ski to raise the load the 8″-plus above the snow or ground. Stephens bolted two pieces of 4″x4″ oak, about three feet in length, to the raised runners as cross pieces to carry the load. He fastened a heavy ring bolt through the center of the front cross member, and uses a short length of light chain, or with small loads, a length of half-inch rope, to secure the load. Purchasing the wood for this could be expensive; you should use what you have or can find. Just make sure it's durable and strong.

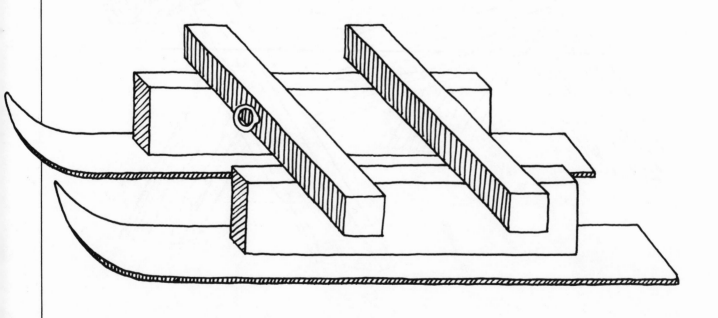

# Stovewood Holder

Beside the woodstove at Garden Way in Charlotte, Vt., sits this stovewood holder. Thanks to an ambitious group of workers, it's rarely seen like this, without wood piled up to its top, ready to be fed into the nearby stove.

Dave Crane of Garden Way Research says a rack like this, built of 1½" or 2¼" pipe, can either be welded or made from plumbing fixtures. The one in Garden Way is about 4' tall and 5' long, with 6" legs so the chips and sawdust that fall from the logs can be swept up from underneath. Make yours to fit in your space for wood storage. It's handier than an old-fashioned woodbox, and neater, too.

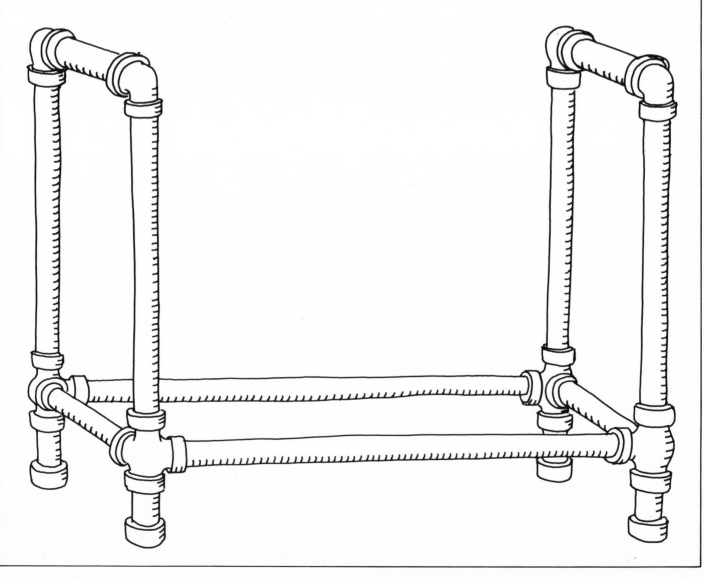

# Wood Box

This "inside-outside" wood box was designed by Peter Coleman, who wrote "*Wood Stove Know-How*" for Garden Way. In a home where wood is being burned it is a must, since it will save miles of carrying each winter for the wood box-filler, it will prevent the loss of heat caused by going in and out during wood-carrying trips, and there will be no tracking in of sawdust, snow and other debris. Peter suggests the inside door be about two by two feet, and up off the floor for easier unloading. The woodbox on the outside must be sturdy, to take the hammering of loads of stovewood. The top should be sloped to let rain water drain off—and the box itself shouldn't be where snow will slide from the roof onto it. Peter also suggests insulating with styrofoam in coldest climates. Insulating the doors inside will do much to keep out the cold. As alternative, roof can be hinged.

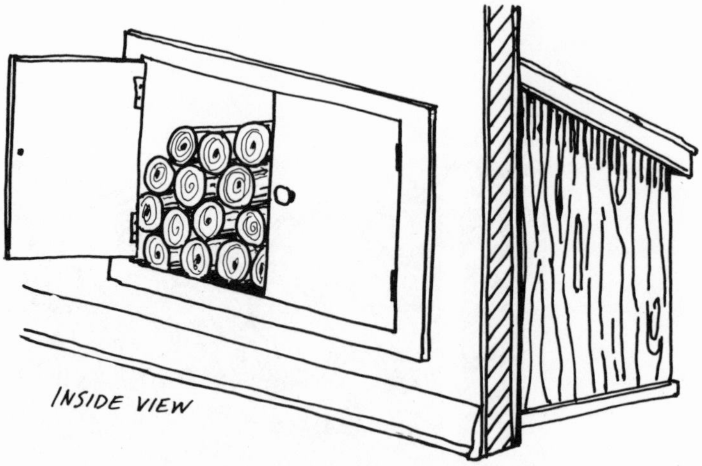

INSIDE VIEW

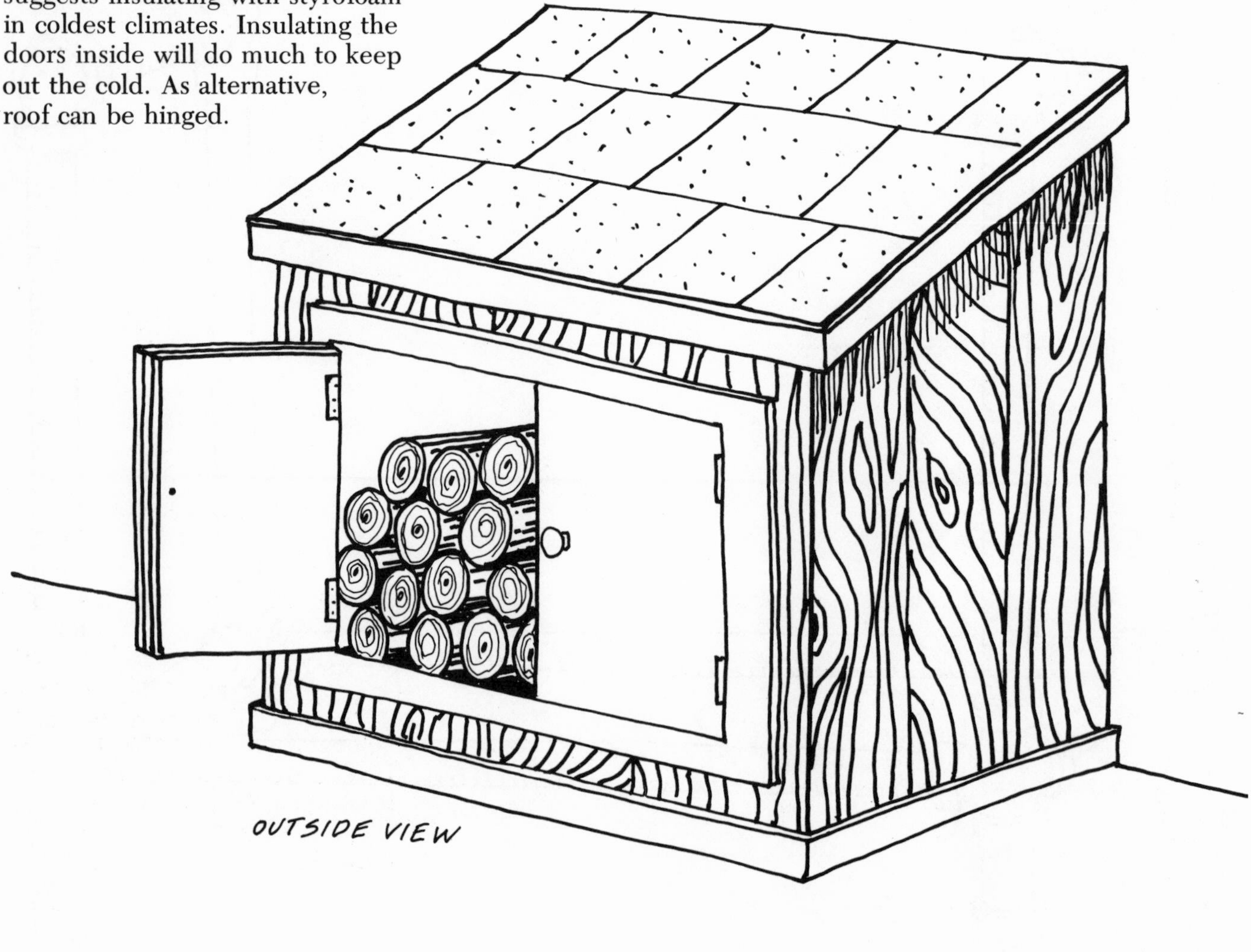

OUTSIDE VIEW

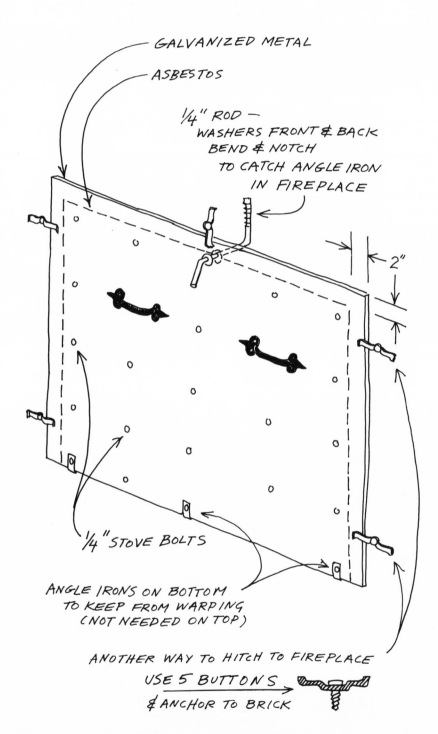

GALVANIZED METAL

ASBESTOS

1/4" ROD —
WASHERS FRONT & BACK
BEND & NOTCH
TO CATCH ANGLE IRON
IN FIREPLACE

2"

1/4" STOVE BOLTS

ANGLE IRONS ON BOTTOM
TO KEEP FROM WARPING
(NOT NEEDED ON TOP)

ANOTHER WAY TO HITCH TO FIREPLACE
USE 5 BUTTONS
& ANCHOR TO BRICK

# Fireplace Front

Bill Nawrath pondered a common fireplace problem. The evening fire was pleasant, but he knew he would have to leave the damper open all night, losing expensive heat.

The next day he built this fireplace front. First he cut a piece of asbestos board exactly the right size to fit the fireplace opening. Then he cut a piece of medium gauge galvanized metal, four inches wider and two inches higher than the asbestos sheet. He lined these up so the two sheets were flush across the bottom, and with a two-inch overhang on the other three sides. Then he fastened the two together, spacing out nine quarter-inch stove bolts and placing a washer on each side of the sheets of each bolt. "Use more bolts if a lighter gauge metal is used," he advises. He also attached two decorative handles near the top.

Bill added a 1″ angle iron on the bottom, with the angle iron giving strength to the asbestos-galvanized metal sandwich and preventing it from warping. This angle iron is drilled so that it can be attached to the fireplace front with ½″ stove bolts.

Bill suggests two ways of attaching this to the fireplace, so that it will be as airtight as possible.

He used a foot-long piece of ¼″ rod bent twice (see illustration) then put through a hole bored in the top center of the metal-asbestos plate so that the rod will stretch up behind the chimney bricks when twisted, thus holding the screen snugly against the fireplace. He used washers on the front and back of the screen to make the crank turn more easily. Another method is to install metal buttons, anchoring them to the fireplace brick as shown in the illustration. Then the screen is put in place and held there with a twist of the four buttons.

# Root Cellar

If you freeze, can or dry the produce of your garden, you'll appreciate a root cellar. It will hold many vegetables in just-picked condition for months, yet is far less work than canning and drying, and cheaper and less work than freezing. And it's possible to consider the storage of bushels of items, instead of quarts.

What's needed for a root cellar?

Very little. It should be spacious enough for your food-saving abilities. Ten feet square is a good family size. It should be insulated off from the rest of the house, so that nearer-to-freezing temperatures can be maintained. And it should have an outside source of air. A window high up on the wall is ideal.

Remember, it's impossible to store all vegetables together. Some require warmth and dryness, some cool, dry air. Aim for providing temperatures as close to freezing as possible, but not below freezing, and as humid as possible.

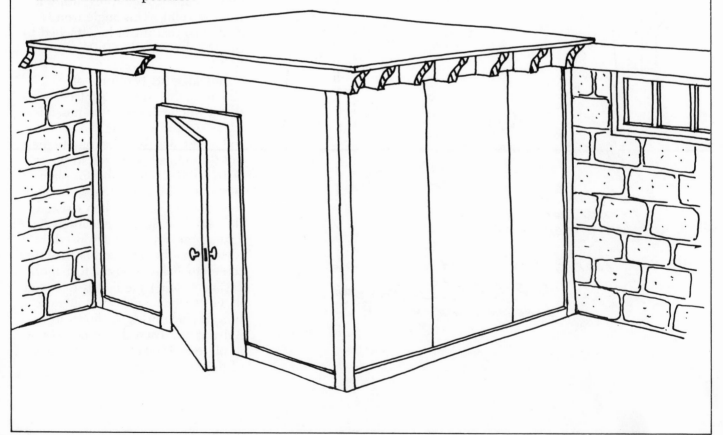

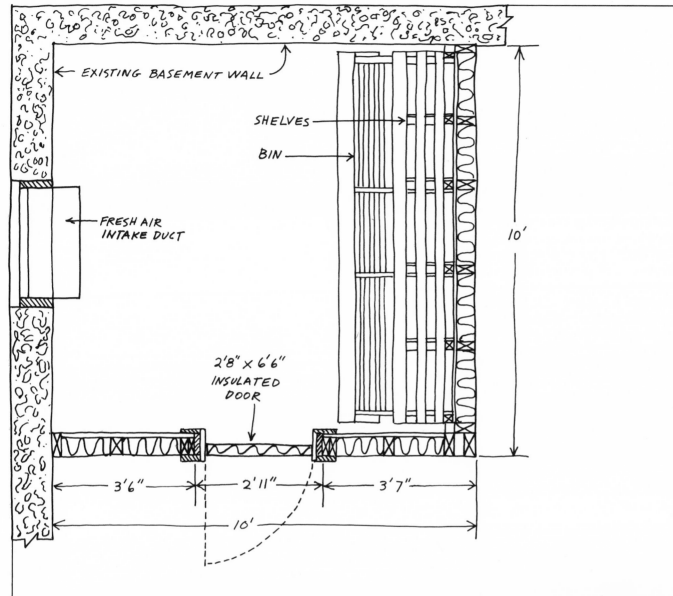

EXISTING BASEMENT WALL

SHELVES

BIN

FRESH AIR INTAKE DUCT

2'8" X 6'6" INSULATED DOOR

3'6"

2'11"

3'7"

10'

10'

Here is the floor plan for a 10'x10' room placed in the corner of a basement. The room has both shelves and slat bins for storage of produce, so nothing is placed on the floor, which is kept damp to increase humidity. Many persons store produce in boxes such as apple crates, believing they are easier to move in and out of the room, and result in less damage to root crops. Boxes should not be placed on the damp floor. This plan is from the Agriculture Canada publication, "Home Storage Room for Fruits and Vegetables," and reprinted by permission.

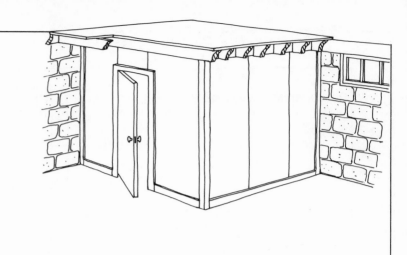

The stress on proper insulation is shown in this cross-section view. Note in walls that the insulation is placed between studs with the vapor barrier on the outside (warm side) to prevent condensation from forming and rendering the insulation ineffective. Agriculture Canada suggests a door made with a 2x2 frame, covered with quarter-inch plywood and insulated with the same material that is used on the wall. The door should fit tightly, open out, and be weather-stripped.

Note details of insulating the ceiling, which again has the vapor barrier on the warm side, in this case nearest the floor above. An easier way to treat the ceiling is to staple a 4 mil polyethylene vapor barrier to the floor joists, making certain there are no air spaces between sheets of the barrier. Then fasten polystyrene or polyurethane board insulation below it with insulation nails.

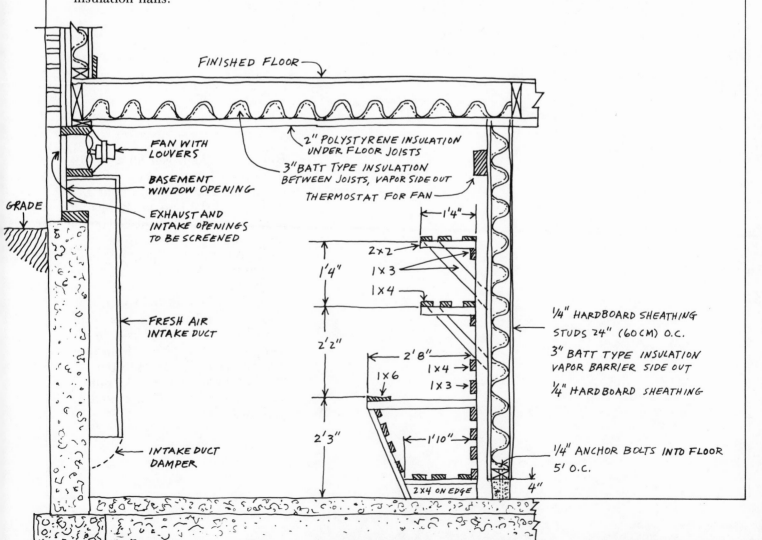

FINISHED FLOOR

FAN WITH LOUVERS

BASEMENT WINDOW OPENING

EXHAUST AND INTAKE OPENINGS TO BE SCREENED

GRADE

FRESH AIR INTAKE DUCT

INTAKE DUCT DAMPER

2" POLYSTYRENE INSULATION UNDER FLOOR JOISTS

3" BATT TYPE INSULATION BETWEEN JOISTS, VAPOR SIDE OUT

THERMOSTAT FOR FAN

2×2

1×3

1×4

1×4

1×6

1×3

1'4"

1'4"

2'2"

2'8"

1'10"

2'3"

2×4 ON EDGE

4"

1/4" HARDBOARD SHEATHING STUDS 24" (60 CM) O.C.

3" BATT TYPE INSULATION VAPOR BARRIER SIDE OUT

1/4" HARDBOARD SHEATHING

1/4" ANCHOR BOLTS INTO FLOOR 5' O.C.

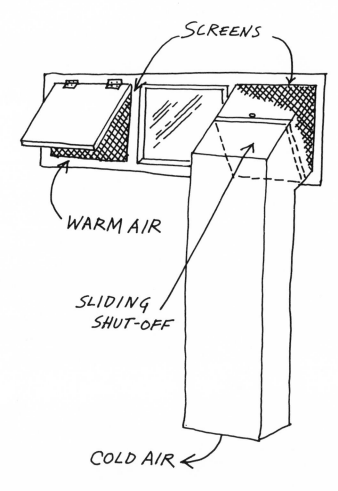

SCREENS

WARM AIR

SLIDING
SHUT-OFF

COLD AIR

The cross-section view of this room shows a fan and louvers set in the upper half of a basement window. These are controlled by a differential thermostat with one bulb inside the room and the other outdoors and out of the sun. This thermostat starts the fan when the outside air is cooler, and will not cut it off until the inside and outside temperatures are nearly the same, or until the inside temperature reaches a pre-selected level. The fresh air intake duct is built to expel air at nearly floor level.

A manual system is shown in the accompanying drawing, with a warm air outlet at left, and floor-level cold air inlet at right. In either case, screens and window coverings should be used to exclude insects and light. In early fall, the system is kept open during cool nights, and is closed during the day.

Here are some rules for using a root cellar:

1. Time your planting of crops for the root cellar so they are as late in the season as possible. Carrots, beets and other root crops can be harvested after the first frost, and will store much better.
2. Store only sound, mature vegetables that show no signs of injury or decay. Root crops should be dry when stored. Don't wash them before storage.
3. If loss of moisture in crops is a problem, store them in plastic bags with small perforations.
4. Check stored crops, and consign to the compost pile any that show decay.
5. To keep humidity high, sprinkle floor occasionally. And to keep boxes of vegetables off damp floor, build slatted duckwalk for them.
6. Clean out root cellar each summer; wash inside and scrub all containers.

# Window Greenhouse

My neighbor started his tomatoes inside, but they were bushy and squat, not the stretchy kind often found in a home setting.

His secret? This "window greenhouse" that keeps his plants out in the sun all day, and protects them from the chills of evening.

He has wooden storm windows, the kind that swing out from the top. And on the south side of his house, he has swung one of them out about two feet from the house. This left a triangle on either side between the window and the house. He constructed two plywood triangles for those spaces. A piece of lumber was cut to fit across the width of the windowsill, and is wide enough to hold level the base of the window box. Side pieces extend from that base out to the window, and on those he nailed the bottom boards, and attached the plywood triangles. The triangles are also fastened to the house with screws. Thus the weight of the project is carried by the base as well as the screws holding the triangles to the house. Hooks and screw eyes hold the window to the bottom of the box.

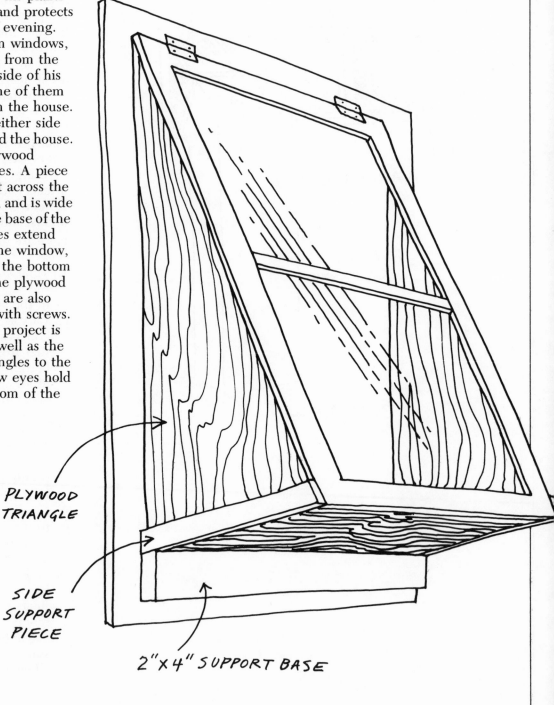

PLYWOOD TRIANGLE

SIDE SUPPORT PIECE

2"x4" SUPPORT BASE

# Outdoor Storage Bins

If your time, ambition or money stops short of a root cellar, there are other possibilities.

One of the easiest is to get a splendid container, courtesy of your friendly town dump. Dumps always have discarded refrigerators. Pick a roomy one, remove the locking latches and the motor and electrical connections. Then dig a hole in the ground, and place the refrigerator in it, door side up, with only a few inches of that top sticking above ground. In the coldest, snowiest climates, you may want to lay a mulch of hay or leaves over the top, so that getting into the refrigerator will be possible all winter, no matter what the weather. All root vegetables can be kept in this, and if you have "keeper" apples, bury a refrigerator just for them, since it will be an ideal spot for them throughout the winter.

Vegetables that can be stored in this include carrots, beets, turnips, salsify and parsnips. Don't store vegetables and fruit together.

Any large containers can be buried in the ground or covered with leaves or hay, and serve as fine root vegetable containers. There are a few simple rules for their use.

1. Place them so moisture drains away from them. A puddle near them will drain into the container and freeze the crops, or will settle around the container and freeze it shut.
2. Use tops on all of them to discourage rodents.
3. Cover heavily with hay or leaves, so the stored goods may be retrieved, no matter what the weather.

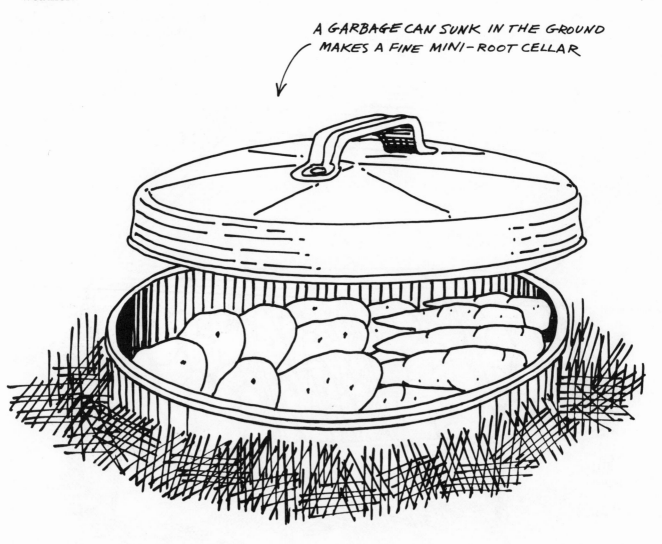

A GARBAGE CAN SUNK IN THE GROUND MAKES A FINE MINI-ROOT CELLAR

BOARD OR
CHICKEN WIRE
TO HOLD STRAW

3 FEET OF
STRAW OR
HAY OR
LEAVES

12 INCHES OF SOIL

A BARREL PIT FOR STORAGE

AFTER EACH LAYER OF VEGETABLES
PACK A LAYER OF STRAW THEN
COVER AND BURY THE BARREL

A more temporary receptacle for root crops can be fashioned from hay bales, placing them so they form a hollow square. If this center hollow is partially filled with hay, any root crops can be stored there safely for several months. This should not be used before brisk fall weather. Try this "container" with a bale or two of hay as a lid. There's one danger of this system. Rodents may share your food.

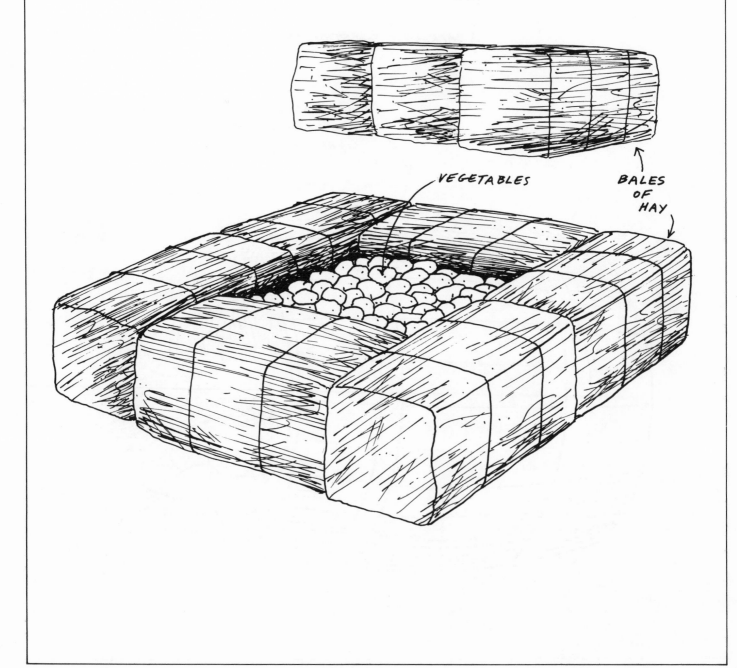

VEGETABLES

BALES OF HAY

To outsmart the rodents, go one step further and build this box that will halt their advances. It's built with a light wooden frame, lined with styrofoam, and has an exterior protective coating of hardware cloth. The top should fit tightly to the box, and, when filled, the box should be covered with a deep layer of hay or some other insulating material. This will make it easy to get into in the winter, even when snow has covered the layer of hay.

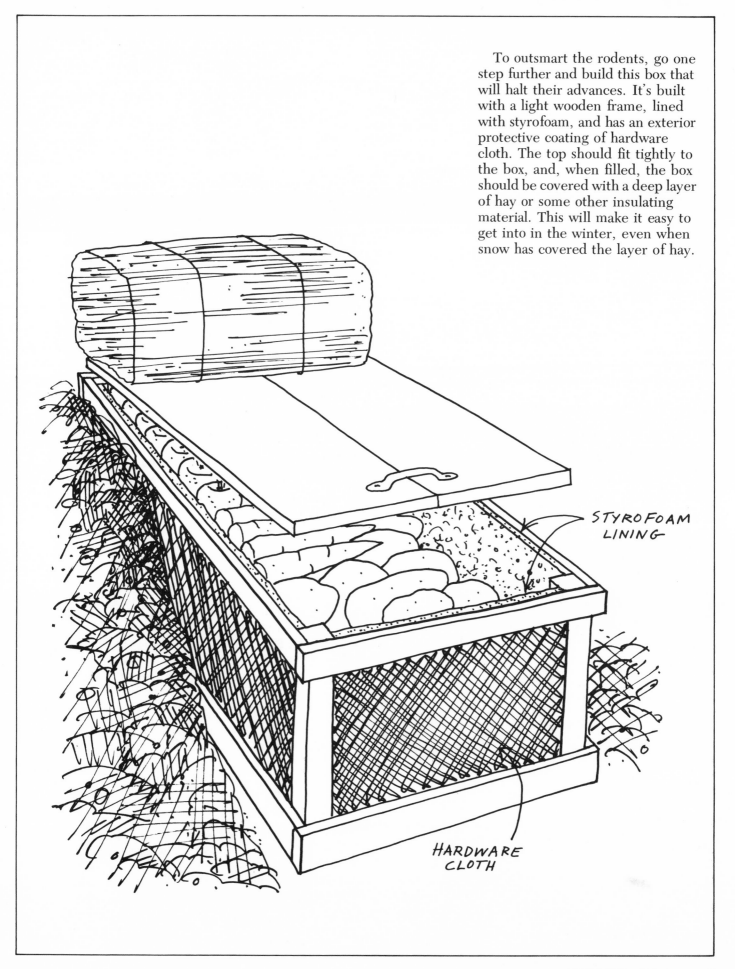

STYROFOAM LINING

HARDWARE CLOTH

Each vegetable has its "ideal" conditions for storage, and of course a compromise is necessary when storing more than one variety.

The following is a table prepared by the Canada Department of Agriculture that lists ideal storage conditions and storage life expectancies.

| Vegetable | Temperature (°F) | (°C) | Relative humidity % | Approximate storage period | Methods for extended preservation |
|---|---|---|---|---|---|
| Asparagus | 32 | (0.0) | 95 | 3 weeks | freeze or can |
| Beans | | | | | |
| green or snap | 45—50 | (7—10) | 85—90 | 8—10 days | freeze or can |
| lima  shelled | 32 | (0.0) | 85—90 | 2 weeks | freeze or can |
| unshelled | 32 | (0.0) | 85—90 | 2 weeks | |
| Beets | | | | | |
| bunched | 32 | (0.0) | 90—95 | 10—14 days | |
| topped | 32 | (0.0) | 90—95 | 1—3 months | |
| Broccoli | | | | | |
| Italian or | | | | | |
| sprouting | 32 | (0.0) | 90—95 | 1 week | freeze |
| Brussels sprouts | 32 | (0.0) | 90—95 | 3—4 weeks | freeze |
| Cabbage | | | | | |
| early | 32 | (0.0) | 90—95 | 3—4 weeks | |
| late | 32 | (0.0) | 90—95 | 3—4 months | |
| Carrots | | | | | |
| bunched | 32—34 | (0.0—1.1) | 95 | 2 weeks | |
| topped | 32—34 | (0.0—1.1) | 95 | 4—5 months | |
| Cauliflower | 32 | (0.0) | 90—95 | 2 weeks | freeze |
| Celery | 32 | (0.0) | 95+ | 3 months | |
| Corn, sweet | 32 | (0.0) | 90—95 | 8 days | freeze or can |
| Cucumbers | 45—50 | (7.2—10) | 95 | 10—14 days | |
| Eggplants | 45—50 | (7.2—10) | 85—90 | 10 days | |
| Endive or escarole | 32 | (0.0) | 90—95 | 2—3 weeks | |
| Garlic, dry | 32 | (0.0) | 70—95 | 6—8 months | |
| Horseradish | 30—32 | (−1.1—0.0) | 90—95 | 10—12 months | can |
| Kohlrabi | 32 | (0.0) | 90—95 | 2—4 weeks | freeze |
| Leeks, green | 32 | (0.0) | 90—95 | 1—3 months | |
| Lettuce (head) | 32 | (0.0) | 95 | 2—3 weeks | |
| Melons | | | | | |
| Cantaloupe or | | | | | |
| muskmelon | 32—45 | (0.0—7.2) | 85—90 | 2 weeks | |
| honeydew | 45—50 | (7.2—10) | 85—90 | 2—3 weeks | |
| watermelons | 36—40 | (2.2—4.4) | 85—90 | 2—3 weeks | |
| Mushrooms | | | | | |
| cultivated | 32 | (0.0) | 85—90 | 5 days | freeze |
| Onion sets | 32 | (0.0) | 70—75 | 5—7 months | |
| Onions, dry | 32 | (0.0) | 50—70 | 5—9 months | |
| Parsnips | 32 | (0.0) | 95 | 2—4 months | |
| Peas, green | 32 | (0.0) | 95 | 1—2 weeks | freeze or can |
| Peppers, sweet | 45—50 | (7.2—10) | 85—90 | 8—10 days | freeze |
| Potatoes | | | | | |
| early-crop | 50 | (10) | 85—90 | 1—3 weeks | |
| late-crop | 39 | (3.9) | 85—90 | 4—9 months | |
| Pumpkins | 45—50 | (7.2—10) | 70—75 | 2—3 months | |
| Radish | | | | | |
| spring, bunched | 32 | (0.0) | 90—95 | 2 weeks | |
| winter | 32 | (0.0) | 90—95 | 2—4 months | |
| Rhubarb | 32 | (0.0) | 90—95 | 2—3 weeks | freeze |
| Rutabaga or turnip | 32 | (0.0) | 90—95 | 6 months | |
| Salsify | 32 | (0.0) | 90—95 | 2—4 months | |
| Spinach | 32 | (0.0) | 90—95 | 10—14 days | freeze or can |
| Squash | | | | | |
| summer | 45—50 | (7.2—10) | 70—75 | 2 weeks | |
| winter | 45—50 | (7.2—10) | 70—75 | 6 months | |
| Tomatoes | | | | | |
| ripe | 50 | (10) | 85—90 | 3—5 days | |
| mature green | 55—60 | (12.8—15.6) | 85—90 | 2—6 weeks | |

# Indoor Storage Bins

Ever need just a handful of soil in the winter—and your garden is down there under two feet of snow? You know the helpless feeling.

Avoid it by storing soil—and sand, peatmoss and any other materials you may need—in bins or cans near your potting bench. A bountiful supply stored in the fall will make the task of starting seeds in the spring an easy one. One Garden Way editor swears by the can cradle shown here, and has five of them for all of the materials he uses to start tomatoes, peppers, flowers and such in the spring. The cradles were built so that 20-gallon metal garbage cans fit into them. You may prefer the storage bin shown here, particularly if you mount each bin on casters, for easier moving.

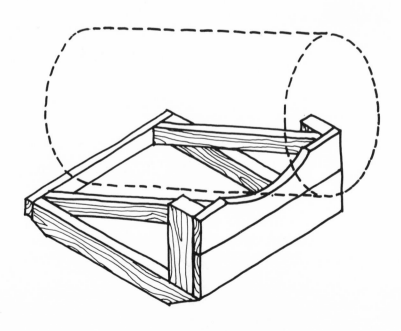

# Tomato Ripening Unit

The sweet-sadness of autumn is summed up in the gardener's plight in raising tomatoes in much of the northern part of this country.

The gardener starts his tomato seeds in March, painstakingly transplants them from flats to tiny pots and then into the garden. He feeds and waters them, desuckers them and ties them. They blossom, they bear healthy green fruit. A few ripen, if he is lucky—then frost threatens.

What to do? He may curse or cry—or take action. And action means picking all of those green and slowly reddening tomatoes, and getting them inside before frost hits. But what can you do with a bushel or two or three of green tomatoes?

Veteran gardeners have found most of them can be eaten and enjoyed if permitted to ripen gradually. This means in a cool and dark (or at least out of the sun) place, and the tomatoes not touching.

In most homes, this is difficult. A bushel of tomatoes, spread out and not touching, simply takes up too much room.

The answer is this tomato ripening unit. It will pay for itself in ripening tomatoes, and is fine for other purposes such as drying onions, beans, seeds and herbs.

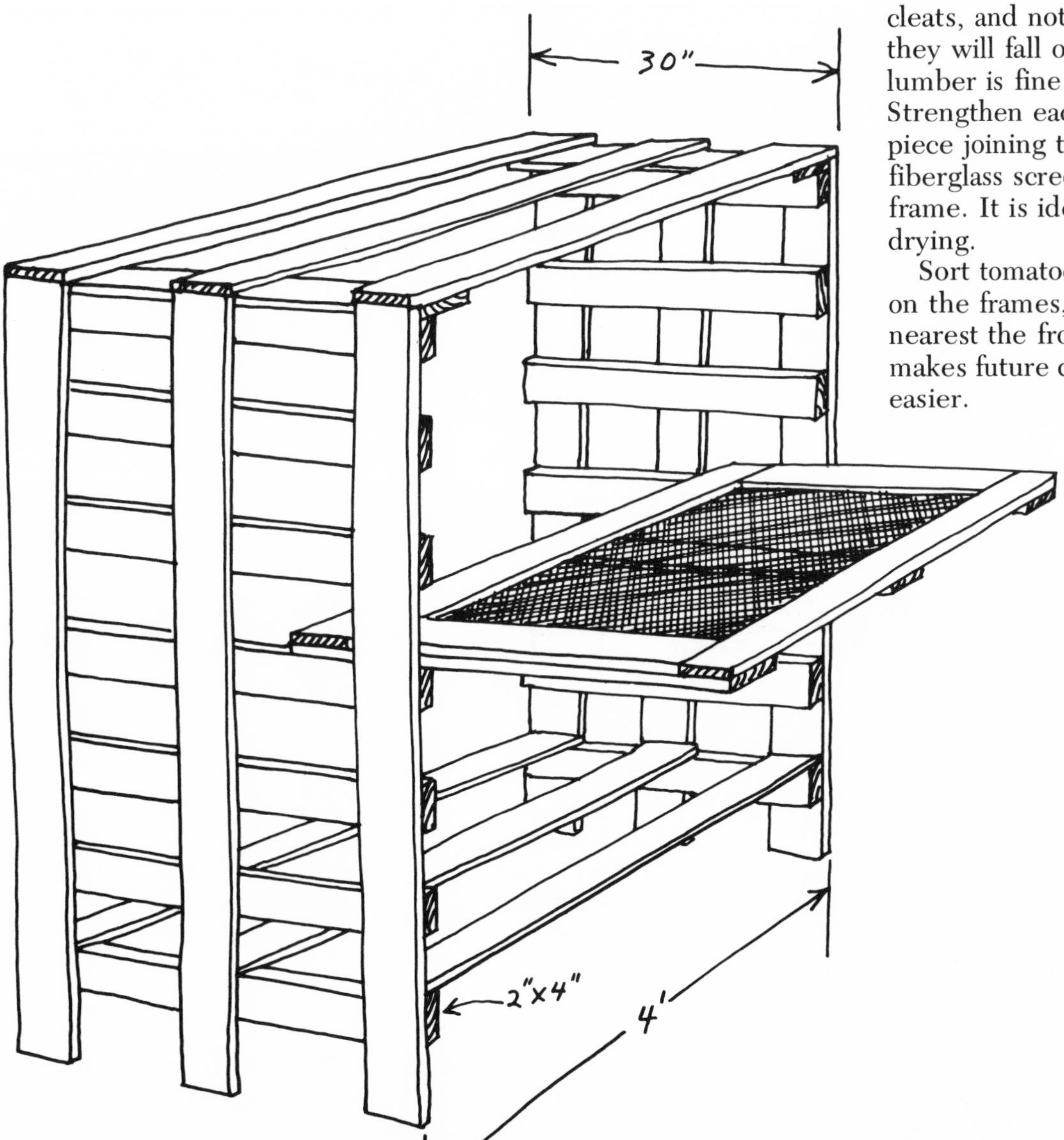

Measure first where you want to place it, and build it to those dimensions. A good working size is 48″ wide by 30″ deep, with space for perhaps five or six racks or trays.

Use 1″x4″ lumber in building frame. Careful with those corners. Make them square, or there will be trouble in fitting the trays. Install 2″x4″ cleats about 8-10″ apart, to give lots of air space, and place the bottom ones at least 8″ off the floor. In building shallow trays to hold tomatoes, measure carefully. Trays must run smoothly along the 2″x4″ cleats, and not be so narrow that they will fall off. Again, 1″x4″ lumber is fine for frames. Strengthen each tray with a center piece joining the front and back. A fiberglass screen is used to cover frame. It is ideal for this, and for drying.

Sort tomatoes as you place them on the frames, with the ripest nearest the front of each tray. It makes future checks on them much easier.

30″

2″x4″

4′

# Solar Drier

In warm, sunny climates, the use of the sun for drying food is practical and inexpensive.

Here's a drier that can be used for fruits and vegetables, and is simple to build and easy to use. Designed by the University of Georgia Extension Service, it is built around a window sash 29″ by 28″. For this size the materials needed are:

1 piece 2″x3″x8′, for legs

1 piece 1″x6″x8′, for side walls of tray

4 pieces 1″x2″x8′, for braces and supports for tray.

Screen wire, boards or fiberglass screen for bottom of tray. Glass top is sloped to get most direct rays from sun.

In less favorable climates, it is often possible to do much of the drying in the sun, then place materials in oven, set at very low heat and with door left ajar, to complete drying process.

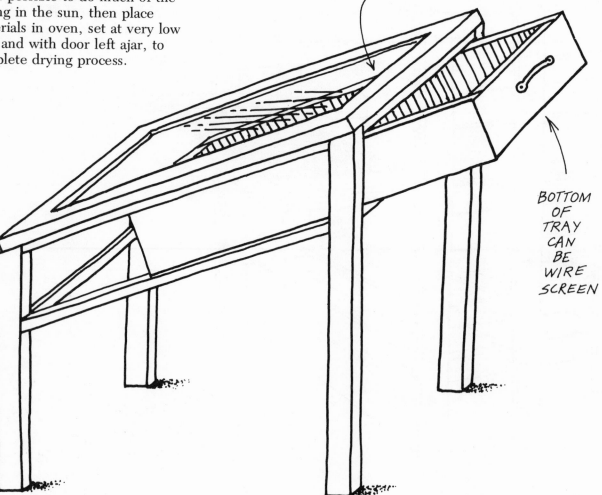

GLASS WINDOW SASH SLOPING TO FACE SUN

BOTTOM OF TRAY CAN BE WIRE SCREEN

# Smokehouse

If you're raising a pig, it's growing fast and you're wondering what you will do with all of that meat, it's time to think of a smokehouse, even if slaughtering time is months away.

Here's an easy one to build. It is inexpensive and roomy. If it works well, you may want to try something more elaborate such as one of those brick buildings of the past.

A few simple truths about smoking meat: You need a cool smoke, since you're smoking, not cooking, the meat. You want a constant but not necessarily tremendous supply of smoke. And you want the smoke to waft past the meat, not hang around. The fuel you select will flavor the meat. Corn cobs are used by some. Hard woods, not completely dried, are used by many. Soft woods, such as pine and spruce, are used by few—and only once. They impart a disagreeable flavor to the meat. And finally, while hams and bacon are the most common meats to smoke, don't be limited to those. Beef, poultry and fish are delicious after being smoked.

This smokehouse, from Wilbur F. Eastman's *The Canning, Freezing, Curing and Smoking of Meat, Fish and Game*, has a smoke chamber made from an old refrigerator. Two holes are cut into it, one at the bottom for smoke to enter, one at the top so smoke will find its way out. The drawing shows a six-inch terra cotta tile smoke tunnel, but stovepipe can be substituted.

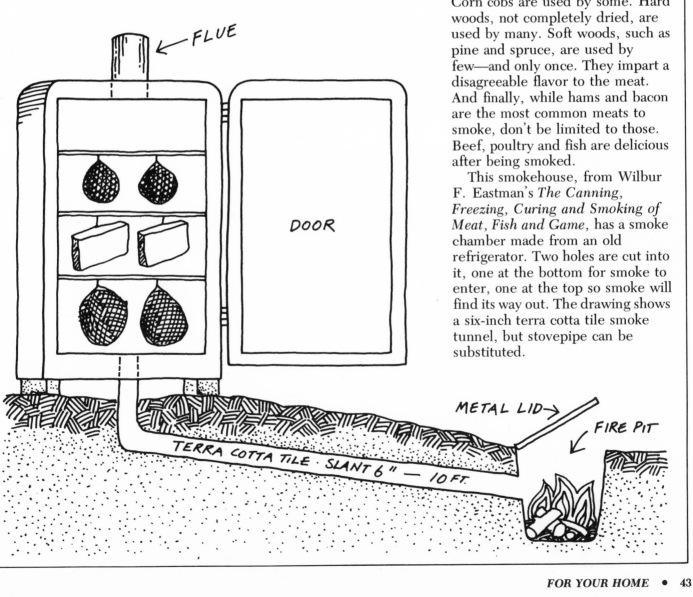

FLUE

DOOR

METAL LID →

← FIRE PIT

TERRA COTTA TILE · SLANT 6" — 10 FT.

# Picnic Bench

There's nothing more pleasant than lunching or dining outdoors in the shade of a tree on a hot summer day. And there's nothing more difficult to store for the winter than that big table and bench on which you dined in such comfort in the summer.

This bench offers two good points. It's roomy, offering eating space for mom, dad and at least four young ones. And in the winter it can be folded up and stored out of the way. Thank the Weyerhaeuser engineers for that.

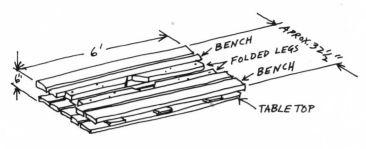

VIEW OF TABLE NESTED FOR
STORAGE OR FOR TRANSPORTING

6'

6"

Aprox. 32½"

BENCH
FOLDED LEGS
BENCH
TABLE TOP

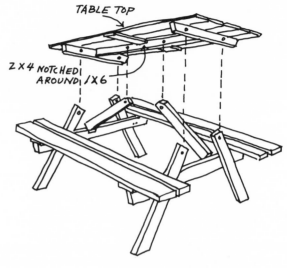

TABLE TOP

2 X 4 NOTCHED
AROUND 1X6

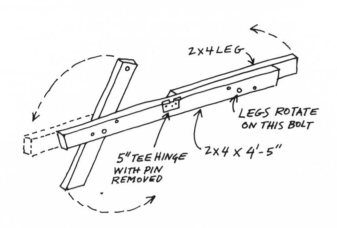

2×4 LEG

LEGS ROTATE
ON THIS BOLT

2×4 × 4'-5"

5" TEE HINGE
WITH PIN
REMOVED

## NOTES

- ALL BOLTS ⅜" DIAMETER
- NAIL FRAME TEMPORARILY FOR DRILLING
- USE WING NUTS ON ALL BOLTS, OTHER
  THAN THOSE MARKED ★, WHICH ARE
  TO REMAIN IN PLACE FOR DISMANTLING
- USE WASHERS ON ALL BOLTS

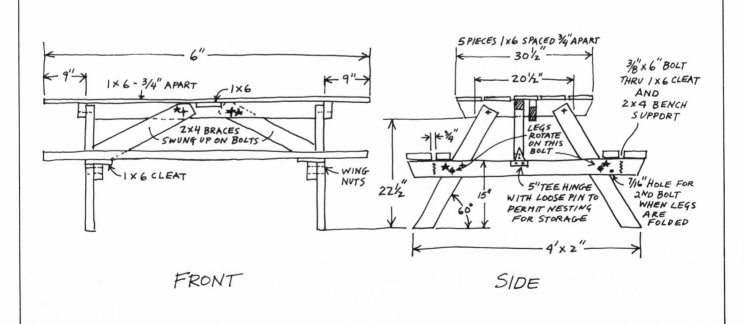

6"

9"

9"

1×6 - ¾" APART

1×6

2×4 BRACES
SWUNG UP ON BOLTS

1×6 CLEAT

WING
NUTS

22½"

FRONT

5 PIECES 1×6 SPACED ¾" APART

30½"

20½"

¾"

LEGS
ROTATE
ON THIS
BOLT

⅜" × 6" BOLT
THRU 1×6 CLEAT
AND
2×4 BENCH
SUPPORT

5" TEE HINGE
WITH LOOSE PIN TO
PERMIT NESTING
FOR STORAGE

7/16" HOLE FOR
2ND BOLT
WHEN LEGS
ARE
FOLDED

15"

60°

4' × 2"

SIDE

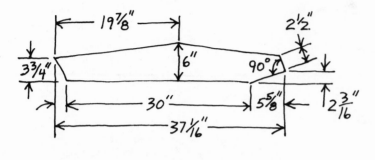

19⅞"

2½"

3¾"

6"

90°

30"

5⅝"

2³⁄₁₆"

37¹⁄₁₆"

2 LEGS

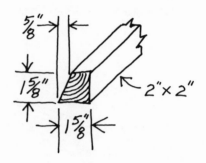

⅝"

1⅝"

2"x 2"

1⅝"

BACK BRACE

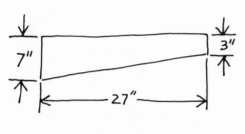

7"

3"

27"

2 ARMS

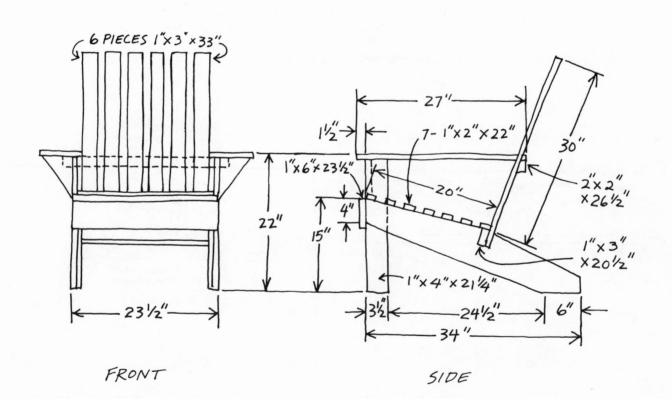

6 PIECES 1"x 3"x 33"

1½"

1"x 6"x 23½"

4"

15"

22"

23½"

FRONT

27"

7- 1"x 2"x 22"

20"

2"x 2" x 26½"

30"

1"x 3" x 20½"

1"x 4"x 21¼"

3½"

24½"

6"

34"

SIDE

# Lawn Chair

If you've ever had the plastic pop under you as you sat in one of those ribbons-and-tubes chairs, you'll appreciate the sturdy comfort of this one, with roomy arms that will hold drink or the book you were reading before you began to nod.

Follow the details closely on cutting the lumber for this one and you'll have no trouble fitting it together. Credit another assist from the Weyerhaeuser people for this design.

# Bootjack

Let's say it's fall and you're thinking already of winter and storing food and lots of wood in the woodshed—and mud and snow tracked into the house, every day and all day. Do something about it. Make this bootjack. Install it right outside the back door, handy for use. And make a place near the back door (inside of course) where the boots can be dropped to dry and be used again. This bootjack can be made in a few minutes and during a winter will save long hours of miserable sweeping and mopping.

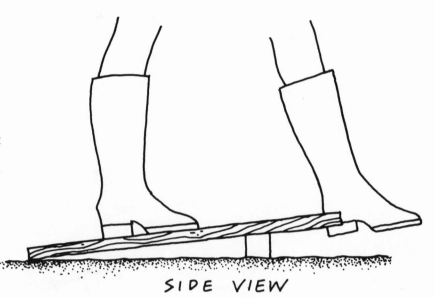

SIDE VIEW

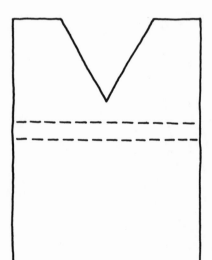

3/4" X 6" X 24"

TOP VIEW

# Mail Box Holder

If mail box holders had to be insured, the rates would be high, since they are stoned by children, hit by cars and snowed under, at the very least, by snowplows.

Here's one that could apply for lower insurance rates. It's set up at an angle that lets it reach out toward the highway. It is swiveled in the center, so it will give a little when hit. And, at 3'8" above the surface of the highway, it's at a comfortable level for that mailman stretching out of his car.

Note carefully that *two* arms reach out from the post, and that the base for the mail box is formed by those two arms plus a block of 2x4 between them. Weyerhaueser recommends nailing arms as well as gluing them to the upright. Countersunk wood screws would do equally well.

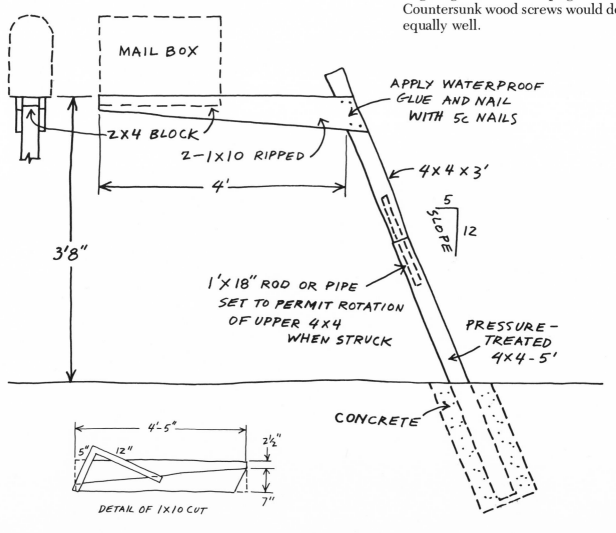

MAIL BOX

APPLY WATERPROOF GLUE AND NAIL WITH 5c NAILS

2X4 BLOCK

2-1X10 RIPPED

4'

4X4X3'

SLOPE 5/12

3'8"

1'X 18" ROD OR PIPE SET TO PERMIT ROTATION OF UPPER 4X4 WHEN STRUCK

PRESSURE-TREATED 4X4-5'

CONCRETE

4'-5"

5" 12"

2½"

7"

DETAIL OF 1X10 CUT

# Hanging Planters

The most effective planters can be constructed at home, easily and quickly. Here are some ideas—and you'll have equally good ones if you think about it.

Here's a simple way to create a hanging planter. Needed, a plastic pot, one of those with the attached saucer is excellent. Heat an ice pick or similar sharp device, then make three holes, spaced the same distance apart, in the saucer lip. Add cord or wire and hang.

How about one with two or even three pots, and made of scrap lumber? Size of pots determines width of lumber needed. For two three-inch pots, a board 1"x6"x12" is used. Cut two holes with diameter the same size as *below* the pot rim. (Remember back in school, how you measured the distance around the pot, divided by 3.1, and got the needed diameter?) Bore holes in four corners for wire or cord for hanging. For a lasting job, paint or use waterproof varnish on this planter. Two pots of Swedish ivy will do you proud in this.

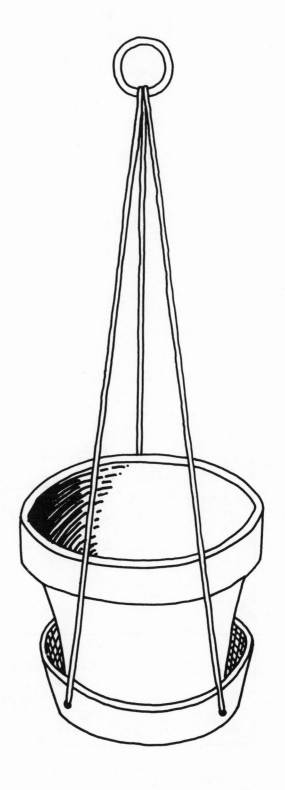

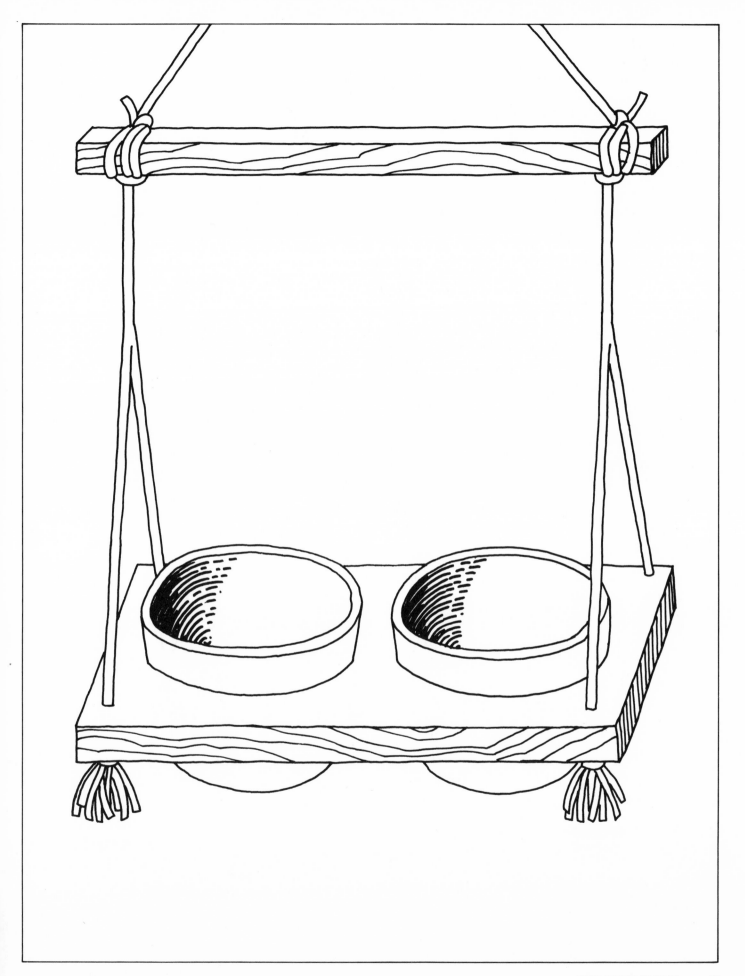

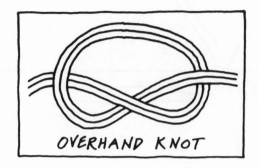

OVERHAND KNOT

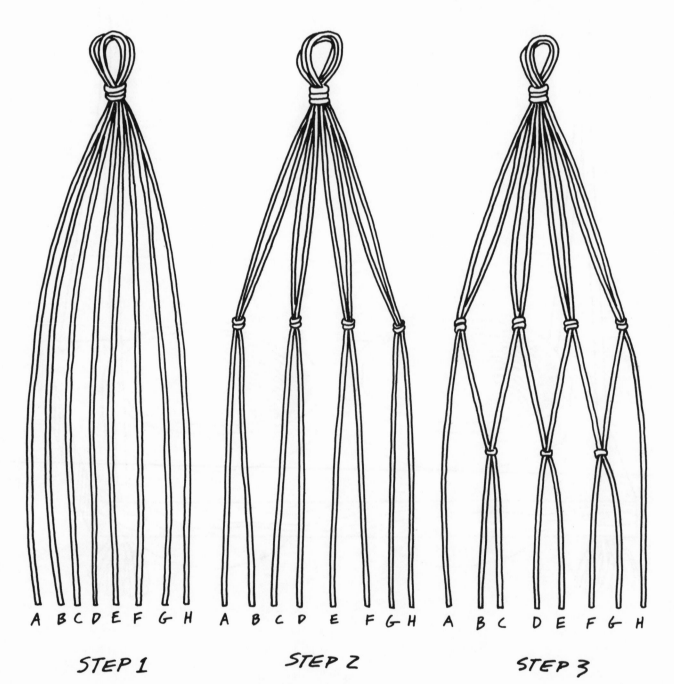

A B C D E F G H

STEP 1

A B C D E F G H

STEP 2

A B C D E F G H

STEP 3

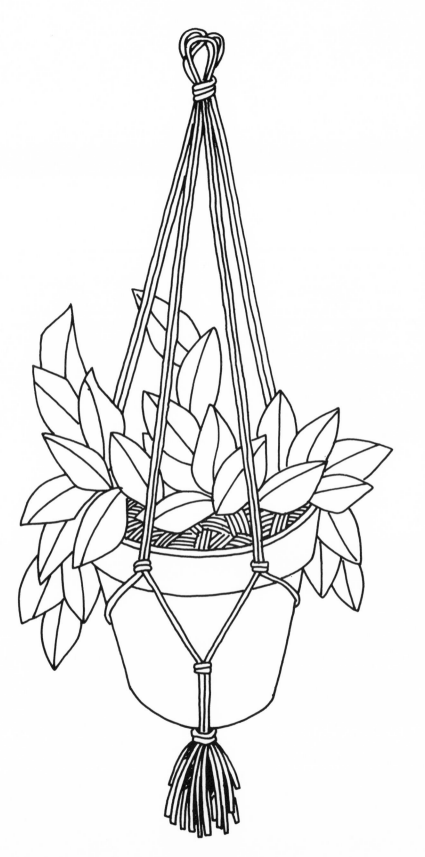

# Macramé Hanger

Discouraged by those prices for macramé hangers? Try your own. Too complicated? Not a bit, if you try this method. If you can tie a shoestring, you can make this hanger. Needed: Four pieces of twine, six feet long. Baling cord is fine for practice. Use nylon cord if you want your work to last without rotting. Double the cords, so all ends are together, then tie a single overhand knot near the folded end of the cords, to provide the loop for hanging. Hang the loop over a hook of some kind, for easier working. Sort the eight strings into four pairs and tie each pair with an overhand knot, halfway between the loop and the end of the strings. These knots should be an equal distance from the end of the strings. In illustration you have tied A and B, C and D, E and F, and G and H.

Ready for the next step? Tie overhand knots halfway between those you just tied and the end of the strings. Tie B and C, D and E, F and G, H and A, thus achieving a circle. Now, as the final step, gather ends of all strings and tie in one overhand knot, forming a tassle. Your flower pot sits on that tassle, and is surrounded by all those strings.

This can be prettied up by using different colored cord, or adding varied colored beads above the knots in various ways. And you will quickly learn to adjust the length of the original cords to the size of the pot you wish to hang, with larger pots requiring longer strings.

# Fluorescent Light Plant Stand

If you crave one of those fluorescent-lighted étagères, but find their price too high, this unit may answer your need. It is inexpensive to build, provides sixteen square feet of growing space, and can be used in many ways. To build it you will need:

4 2"x4"x72" uprights

9 2"x2"x48" horizontal pieces

4 1"x6"x48" sides of plant area

1 48"x48" particle board or plywood shelf

1 60"x60" plastic sheet shelf covering

2 48" two-tube fluorescent units, with hooks and chains

Optional

1 2"x2"x96" to be cut into four supports

This unit is excellent for a basement where vegetable plants such as tomatoes, peppers and cabbages can be started. The lighting units are hung on chains, and can easily be held in a raised position, while you are watering plants or caring for them, with S-hooks. Height of the light units can also be changed by altering lengths of chains held by hooks at the top of this unit.

Use wood screws throughout. Construct frame shelf and end units, then place shelf at a height comfortable for you. Two top bars are screwed into position, and steel hooks are screwed into them in a position so that light units hanging from them will be centered properly. Shelf is then constructed on frame, and 1"x6" side pieces are added. The plastic sheet is placed within this unit. If it is filled with peat moss and the peat moss is kept dampened, the humidity of the air around your plants will be raised. While most persons will use this as a place to start vegetables, it is equally valuable for houseplants.

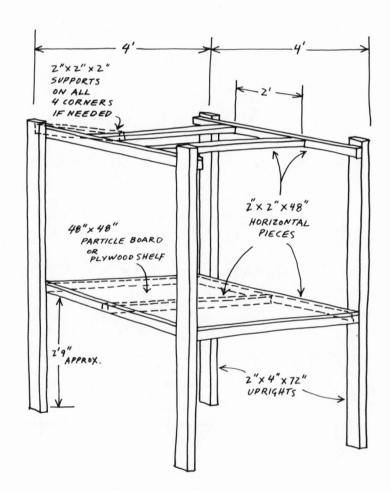

PLANT STAND STRUCTURE
BEFORE ADDITION OF
FLUORESCENT LIGHTS
& PLANT AREA BOX

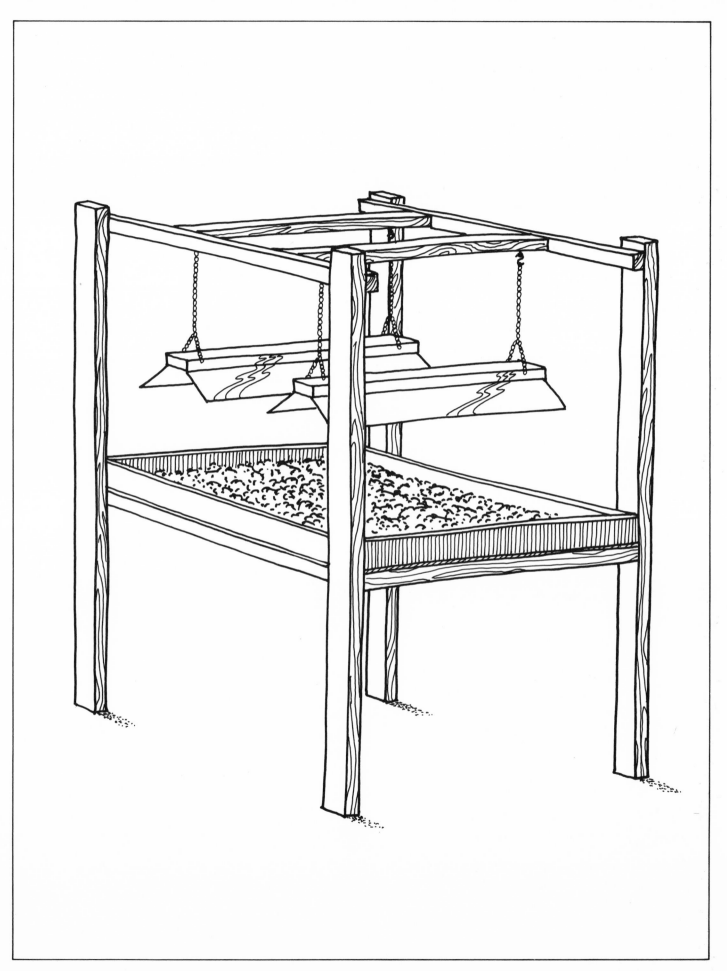

# Part 2

# EASY-TO-MAKE THINGS FOR YOUR GARDEN

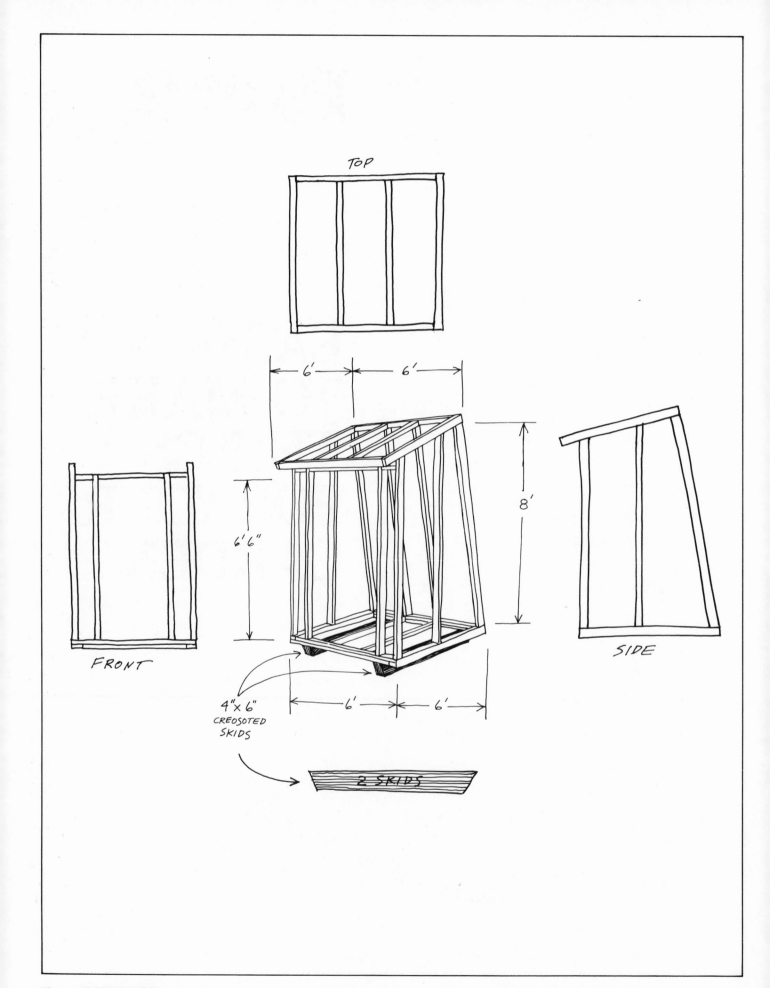

TOP

6' | 6'

8'

6' 6'

FRONT

SIDE

4"x 6"
CREOSOTED
SKIDS

6' | 6'

2 SKIDS

# Tool Shed

Garden tools need proper care if they are to serve long and well. In the following pages are some ways to keep them ready for work.

The first need is to provide a roof over their heads. If you want something that is easy to obtain and will do well, buy one of those metal sheds of which there are so many on the market.

If you want something a little special, consider this one, designed by Douglas Merrilees. It can be finished on the outside so that it has the same exterior as your home, or has an exterior that blends well with your home.

Note that it is built on 4"x6" creosoted skids. While this means it can be moved, such a move isn't something you will want to try every day, since this is heavy. The other benefit of building this on skids is that the floor is raised well off the ground, virtually eliminating the problem of moisture gradually eating away the bottom of the building. An alternative is to build it on a concrete block base.

While this one is 6' by 6' at the base, you of course can design your own to fit your needs. A law of gardening applies here: no matter what size you build it, you will fill it with tools and other supplies.

# Tool Storage

Gardening chores are completed much more quickly and in a better frame of mind if tools are readily available. If a hunt for a hoe must precede hoeing the peas, the work becomes a chore. No better way to avoid such troubles than by creating a place for each tool. A rack is shown in the illustration that will please you. A simpler way is also illustrated.

The rack is a much more professional job, is efficient and long-lasting. The simpler way, a piece of lumber nailed across the studs of a garage or barn, has the sole virtue of being quick to achieve.

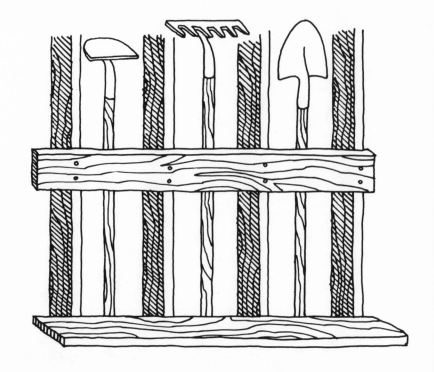

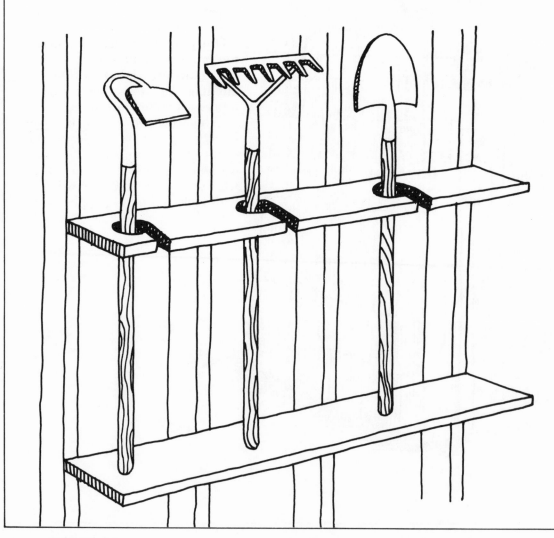

# Tool Sharpening

Your hoe need not be "dull as a hoe," and it will chop weeds more easily if it is sharpened properly. An eight-inch mill file is good. Use vise to hold hoe. Stroke toward cutting edge, as shown. Unlike shovel, with blade that is centered, hoe has cutting edge on side nearest handle, and this should be maintained.

A sickle, like a hoe, is sharpened on only one side. With the sickle, bottom side of blade remains flat, with file applied only to upper side of blade.

CAUTION: Of all blades to be sharpened, sickle blade may be the most difficult to complete without cutting your own fingers. Work carefully and slowly.

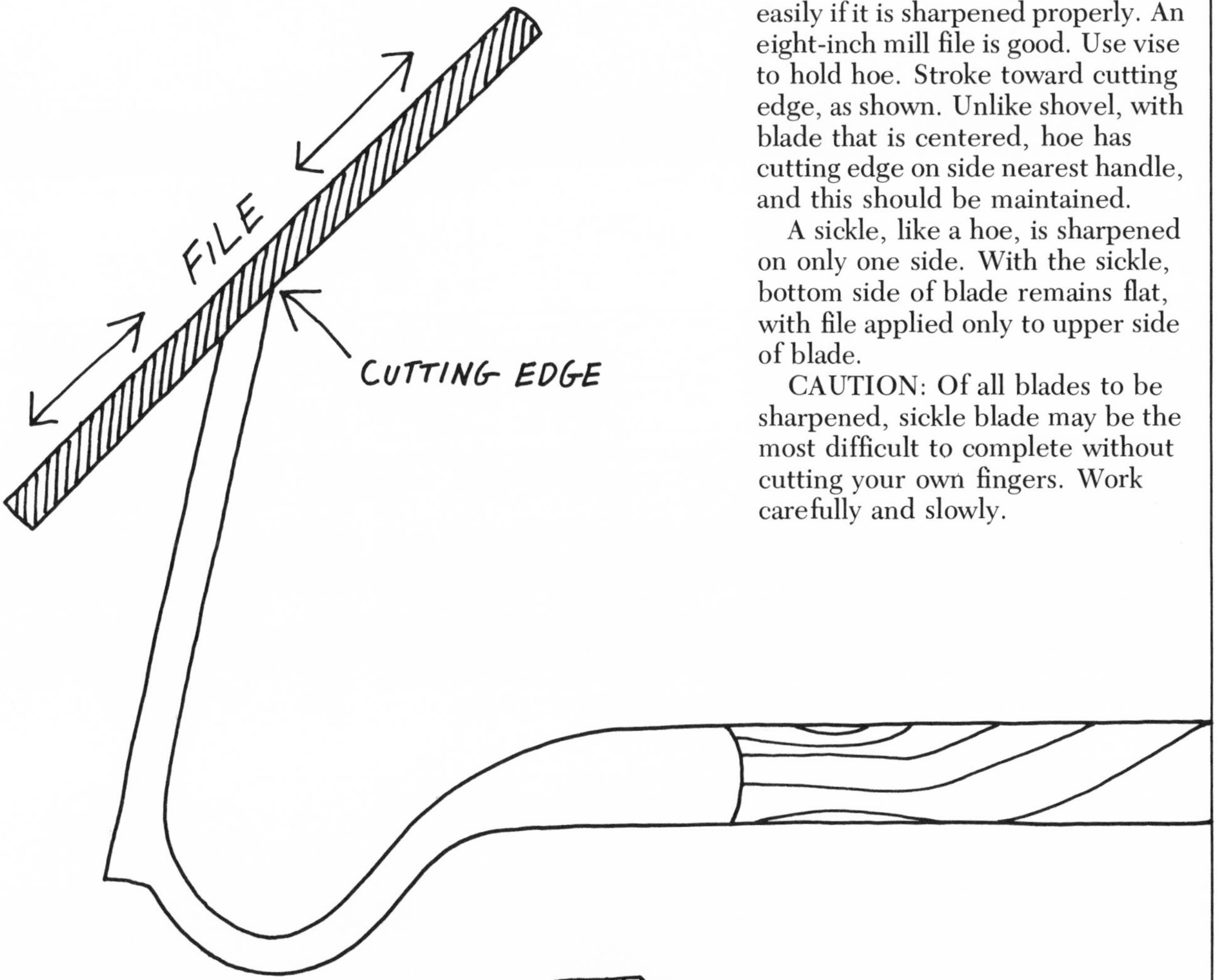

FILE

CUTTING EDGE

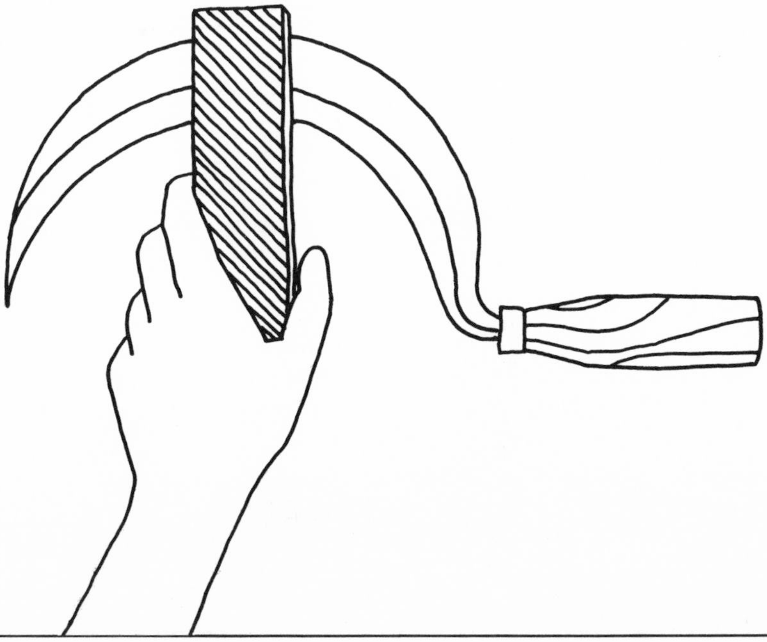

# Tool Cleaner

Here's a project that can be completed as quickly as you can read about it. Take an old container, a box or a roomy pail. Fill it with sand, then dump in some oil, and used crankcase oil will work just as well as any other kind. Place this near your tool storage area. When you're finished for the day with a shovel or hoe, push it down into the sand and work it around a bit. It will come out cleaned, and with a coating of oil to resist the rust. If your tools are rusty before using this for the first time, clean them once, well, and you'll never have to clean them again. For the final cleaning, use a wire brush or steel wool and get off all of that rust that can shorten their useful lives by so many years.

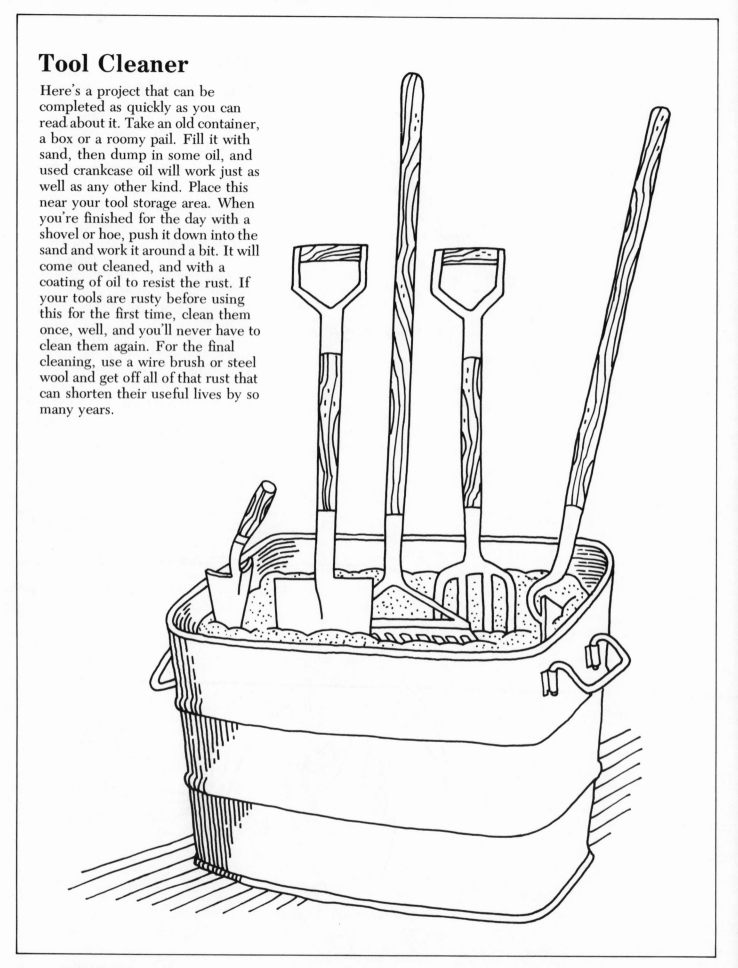

# Tool Finder

If you are one who never misplaces a garden tool, this item is not for you. But if you do occasionally use a trowel, and put it on the ground "just for a minute," here's some advice. Paint the handles of all such tools. Use a brilliant color—yellow is great—and they'll stand out, reminding you to pick them up. Such coloring is also valuable when a small tool actually does get misplaced down among green plants. It will save a long and irritating solo game of hide-and-seek.

ENAMEL
RED

# Tool Brander

For quick identification of your tools, and to increase the chances of having the borrowed ones returned, borrow an idea from the West, and brand them, partner. You don't need a branding iron for this method.

Scrape or sandpaper a spot for the brand on the lower part of tool handle, to remove any dirt, paint or varnish. Print your initials on the spot with fingernail polish, then quickly light that polish with a match. It will char the initials into the handle. If initials are faint, repeat process.

Careful with that flame and bottle. The polish is highly flammable.

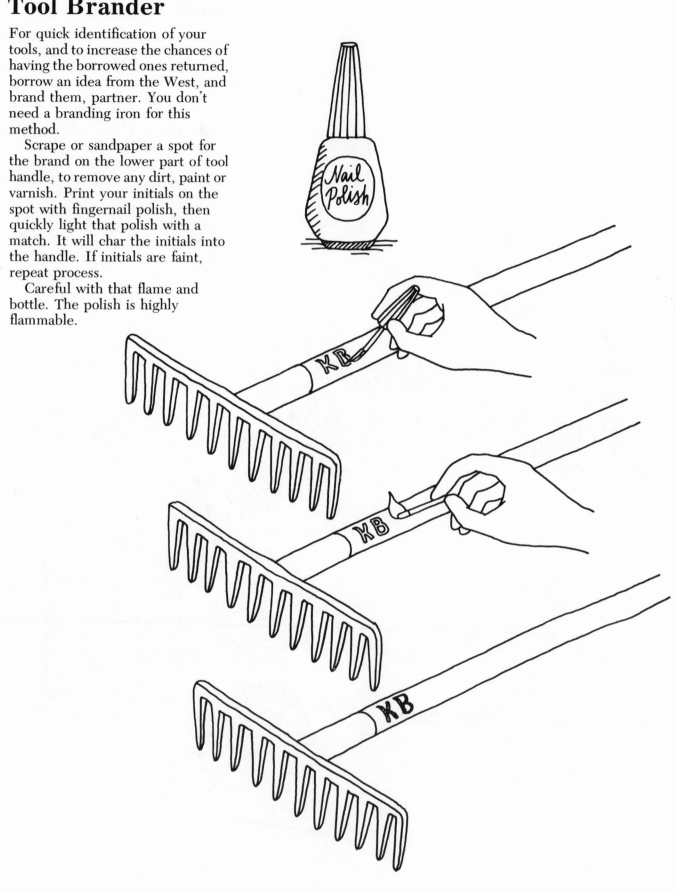

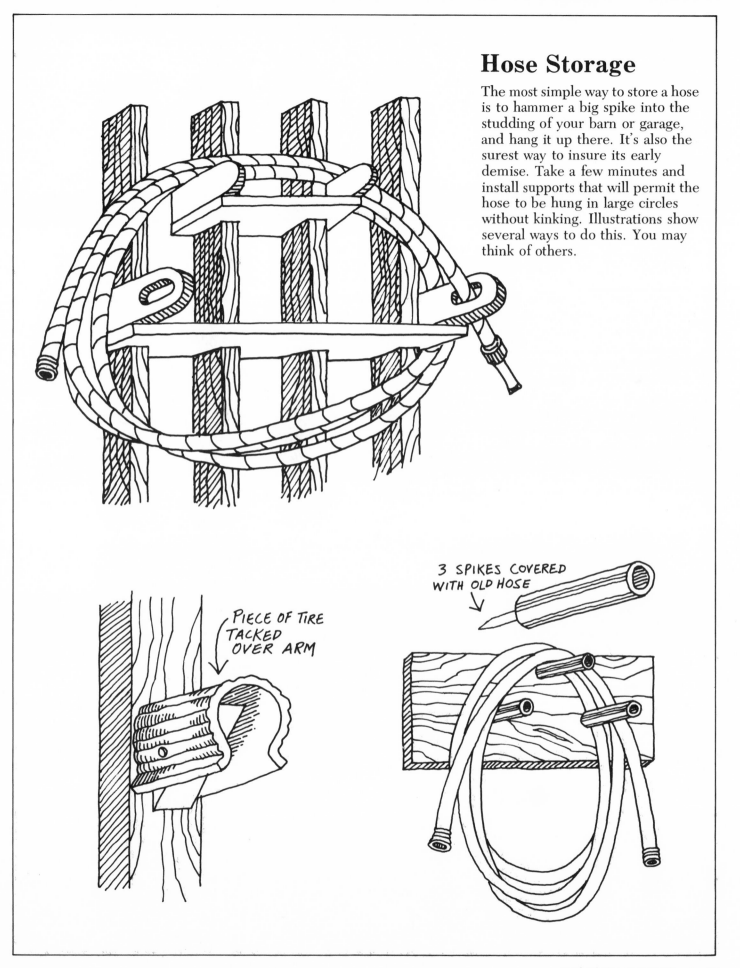

# Hose Storage

The most simple way to store a hose is to hammer a big spike into the studding of your barn or garage, and hang it up there. It's also the surest way to insure its early demise. Take a few minutes and install supports that will permit the hose to be hung in large circles without kinking. Illustrations show several ways to do this. You may think of others.

PIECE OF TIRE TACKED OVER ARM

3 SPIKES COVERED WITH OLD HOSE

# Handy Box

This is a garden handy box, to be put up on a post near the garden entrance. It will hold the many things you may now carry in your pockets—string for lining up rows and a trowel—plus the things you have to go back to the house for—a salt shaker for discouraging the cabbage moths, a duster of rotenone, rubber knee pads worn for the fine weeding, a section of old sheeting to be torn up for tomato ties. Make this about mailbox size. If it's too big it will just get cluttered and useless. Save space in it for a notebook with your garden plan and planting schedule in it, and a pencil to jot down when you planted what and where. Make it waterproof. Soon you'll find you're saving many unnecessary steps.

## Tea, Garden Style

Here's a must for every garden. Wheel a 55-gallon oil drum, or some container as large as possible, into a corner of the garden. Fill it one-fourth full of manure or compost. Or put manure or compost into burlap bag and hang in drum. Fill drum with water. Stir occasionally. In a few days this will brew into a rich, brown tea, great for reviving transplanted plants, or for sickly plants, or just to stimulate the growth of any crop. For a few times it's possible to replace tea with water, until product begins to lose character. Then replace compost or manure and start again.

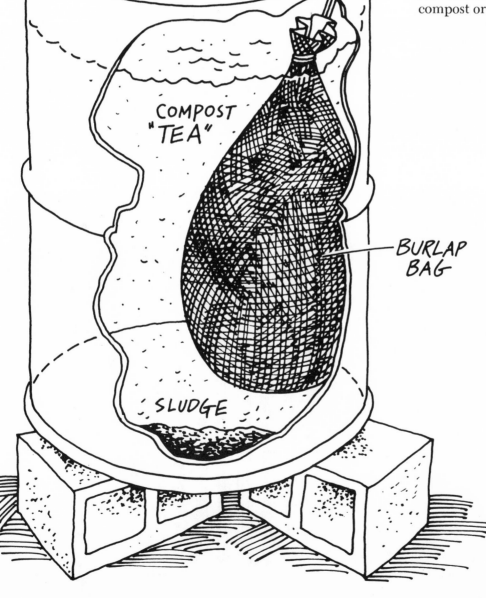

COMPOST "TEA"

BURLAP BAG

SLUDGE

# Compost Materials

One of the joys of composting is finding the organic material needed to build the pile. Almost anything organic will do, and the greater the variety the better the pile. Most books list spent hops, felt wastes and olive residues—materials most of us don't trip over every day. But there are many for the asking, including garden refuse, leaves and garbage.

I sat in the local barber shop, pondering my compost pile and watching long, white locks pile up around the chair, for I had been unshorn too long. I recalled something I had read the previous evening in a Rodale book, that six or seven pounds of human hair contain a pound of nitrogen, which is the much-needed ingredient in all compost piles.

"Bill," I asked the barber, "what do you do with all this hair?"

He looked startled. "Are you saying you want your hair back?"

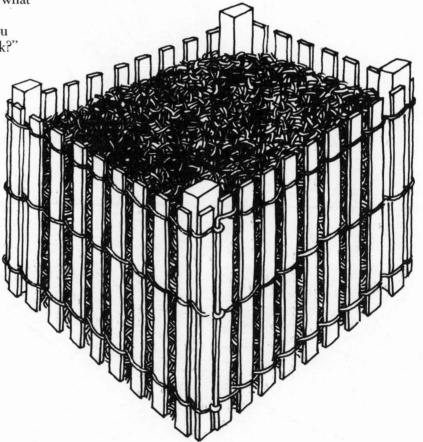

I muttered something, but not in time. "Hey, Jim," he called to his partner busily snipping nearby, and in a voice that made all waiting customers look up, "he wants to save his own hair."

Ever try hiding under a barber's bib, while he's cutting your hair?

The list of material that can be composted is endless, since all organic material can be added to the pile. Some of the more common ones are lawn clippings, spoiled hay, garden trash, garbage, wood ashes, leaves, manure—the list goes on and on.

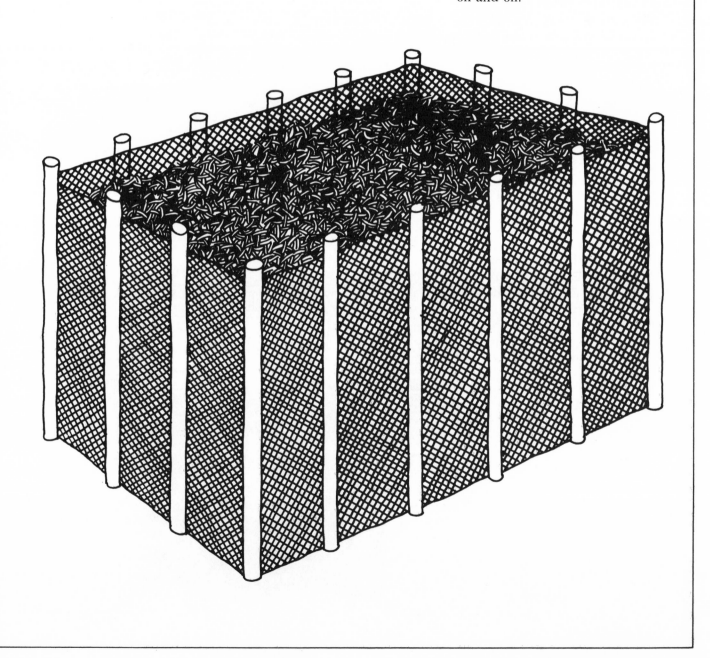

# Compost Piles

The construction of bins to house the compost pile ranges from staking up circles of chicken wire to the careful building of concrete block or brick structures.

The most simple is often the best. That circle of mesh permits air circulation around the pile, and is easy to move when the gardener wishes to turn the pile and speed its decay.

Points to remember:

1. The ideal size is six feet wide, three to five feet high and any length, beyond six feet.
2. Walls should not exclude air, or the aerobic (with air) bacterial action of breaking down the organic matter will be halted.
3. Place the pile close to the garden, which is the source for much of the composted material and where most of the compost will be used. A shady spot near a water supply is ideal.
4. Compost as much material as you can find. The pile will shrink to about half its original size—and there's no such thing as too much compost.

For fast results, a series of three bins, made from chicken wire or a heavier mesh, is recommended. It permits the gardener to start the compost in one pile, turn it over into the next, and finish it in the third bin, meanwhile starting other piles in the first bin. Such a continuous process will speed the composting and increase the amount of compost.

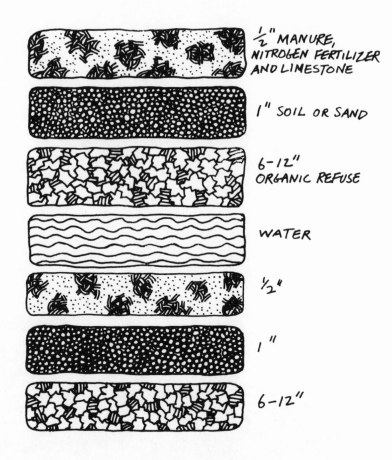

½" MANURE, NITROGEN FERTILIZER AND LIMESTONE

1" SOIL OR SAND

6-12" ORGANIC REFUSE

WATER

½"

1"

6-12"

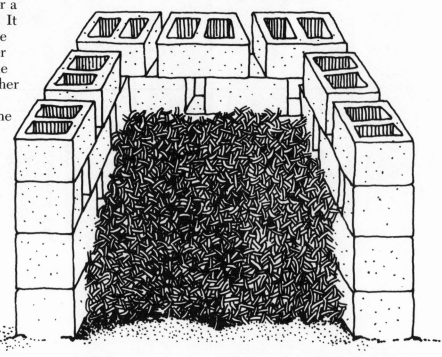

# Two-Bin Composting

Stu Campbell, author of *Let It Rot*, suggests this two-bin container is both practical and long-lived. Concrete blocks are held in place with mortar, and the blocks are set on edge with the holes open to allow free passage of air. Boards are put in place as the pile builds up. Best use for this model would be to build up a pile in the first bin, let it "cook" for several weeks, then shovel it into the second bin for final composting, while building up another pile in the first bin.

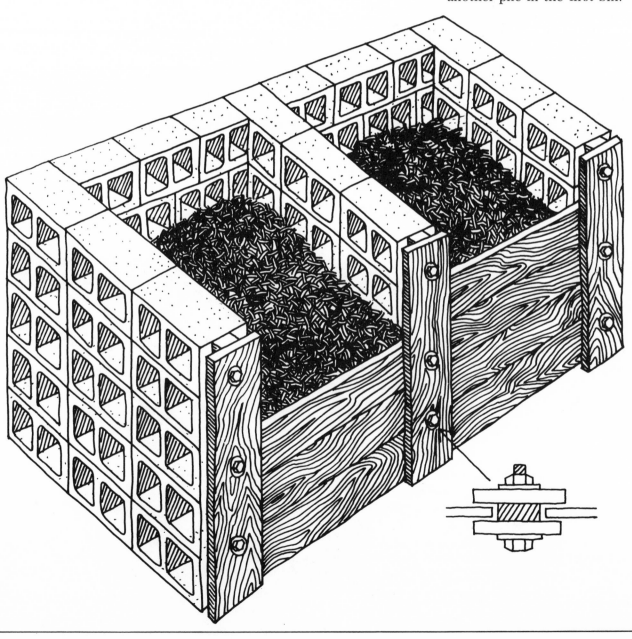

# New Zealand Compost Box

Stu Campbell explains that this box requires two pieces of 2″x2″x10′ (to be cut into six pieces of 2″x2″x39″) plus twelve pieces of 1″x6″x8′ to be cut into twenty-four pieces, each 48″ long. The uprights are dug three inches into the ground and the sideboards are spaced a half-inch apart, to permit air circulation. The front boards, which slide in and out, make the work of filling and emptying the box much easier. We would recommend longer uprights, and more side pieces. Thus a higher pile could be built. It will soon settle back to three feet, even if the makings are piled five feet high originally.

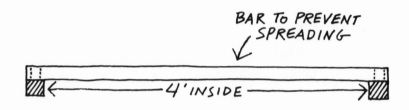

BAR TO PREVENT SPREADING

4′ INSIDE

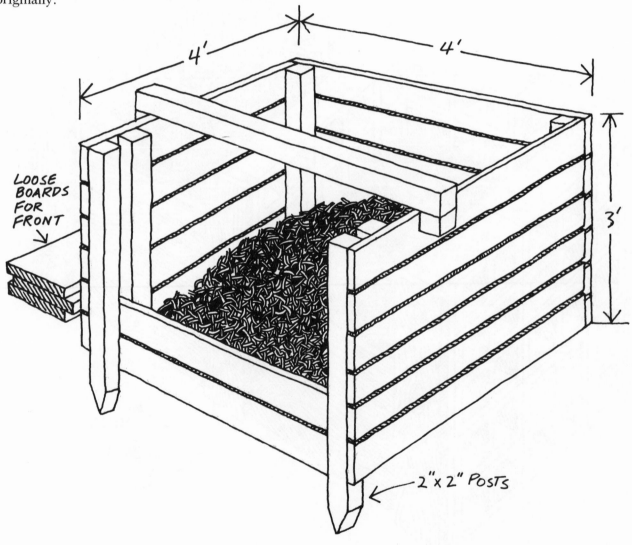

4′

4′

3′

LOOSE BOARDS FOR FRONT

2″x 2″ POSTS

# Handy Composter

Here is a model of a compost bin that has been used for many years and was designed by Lyman Wood. Most people advise placing a compost pile in an inconspicuous place, but this is one you won't mind a bit having your visitors see, particularly if it is full of the rich, black results of composting.

Using 2x2 or similar wood, make four frames, each four feet high and six feet wide. Reinforce the corners with 2"x2"s as shown. Cover each with chickenwire—the half-inch mesh will hold its shape longer than the cheaper and larger meshes. The originator of this bin linked these panels into two L-shaped sections that were linked into a square with screen door hooks. Another Garden Wayer has found it easier to handle the panels if all are linked with the screen door hooks, two to each corner, rather than forming the L-shaped sections.

Either way, this is an easy bin to use—easy to assemble, and particularly easy to use when the pile should be turned. First take the sides apart, then reassemble it beside the compost pile, and fork the pile back into the bin.

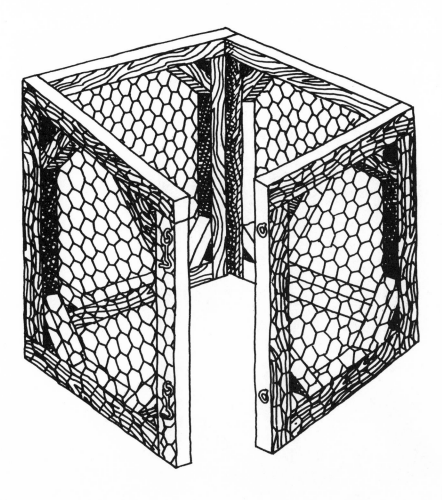

# Simple Compost Bin

This has to be the most simple compost bin to build—and one of the most effective to use. Find strong wire mesh—four or five feet wide is good. Cut a section nine feet long. Wire the two ends together, forming a circle. Fill it with composting material. When it's time to turn the pile, remove the wire, set it beside the pile, then fork the pile back into the wire frame, remembering of course to place the outer, uncomposted material into the center of the pile this time.

# Cold Frames

Imagine moving your garden 300-400 miles south each spring and fall. That's about what a cold frame or hotbed can do for your gardening effort. By using one or both of them you can extend your growing season four to six weeks on each end.

Beginners should start first with a cold frame. It's cheaper both to build and, unless the old fermenting manure heating method is used, easier to operate than a hotbed. And it's a good teacher. You will learn, quickly, the tricks of controlling this tiny environment to your advantage.

Some gardening books will tell you to build frames of concrete or concrete block. This is fine, but only if you are absolutely sure of your site and of the size you want. Better to build first with wood, so that any error can be rectified easily.

Start modestly, with a single bed of 6'x3' dimensions. This will give you the feel of working with a cold frame, and its possibilities in your area. Such a modest beginning, too, will give you valuable insight into the correct location and construction of more ambitious frames, tailored to your location and needs.

Here is a good model to begin with. It's simple to build, small enough so that even a short-armed person can reach into all areas of it, but large enough to help in your gardening.

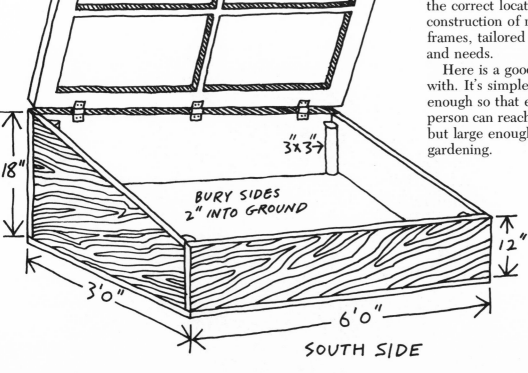

3'X 6' COLD FRAME SASH

3"X3"

18"

12"

BURY SIDES 2" INTO GROUND

3'0"

6'0"

SOUTH SIDE

These two diagrams show another cold frame that is easy to construct, using two 3'x4' storm sashes. If you make your own sash for this you might try plastic wire screen cloth which is much more durable than the plastic often used. In building the cold frame, use redwood or cypress if available, otherwise soak wood with preservative. Use of loose pin hinges makes it easier to remove sash for repainting or when not in use.

Here are some basic points about the design, construction and use of the cold frame.

*FRAME:* Use 2"x4" for the corner stakes, or better yet, cut 3"x3" diagonally for these stakes, providing enough strength without intruding as much into the cold frame area. For the frame itself, get 1"x12" rough lumber, cut it, coat it with a wood preservative, penta not creosote, then paint it. Find or purchase sash, then build the frame to fit it. The dimensions shown, 18" in rear and 12" in front, are ideal, both for permitting the runoff of rainfall and for maximum sun in the cold frame.

*SASH:* There are several possibilities. Best, easiest but most expensive is purchase of it. Standard sizes are 3x6, 3x3 and 2x4. Another possibility is using old storm windows, which are usually cheap and available, and are usually 2½'x4½'. Third possibility is to build your own, using either glass or heavy plastic. Plastic is not as durable as glass and should be reinforced to stand the stress of snow or wind.

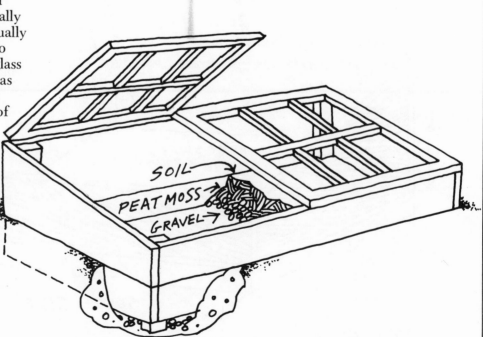

SOIL

PEAT MOSS

GRAVEL

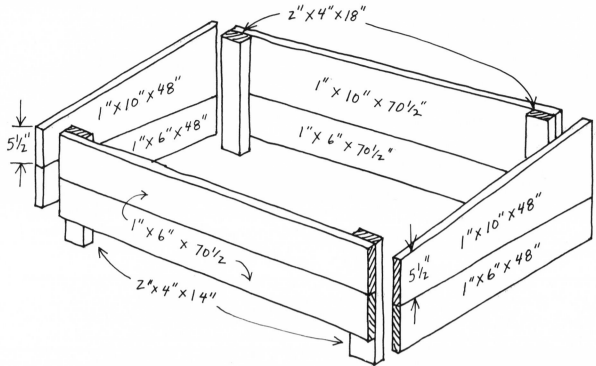

2" x 4" x 18"
1" x 10" x 48"
1" x 10" x 70½"
1" x 6" x 48"
1" x 6" x 70½"
5½"
1" x 10" x 48"
5½"
1" x 6" x 48"
1" x 6" x 70½"
2" x 4" x 14"

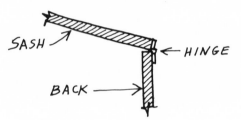

SASH
HINGE
BACK

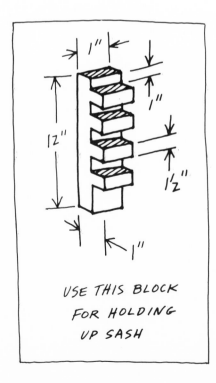

1"
1"
12"
1½"
1"

USE THIS BLOCK
FOR HOLDING
UP SASH

*SOIL:* If your soil is rich, simply place the cold frame where you want it, in a slight trench so the bottom of the frame is at least one inch below the surface. But if conditions are less than ideal, dig out a one-foot layer from the site. If drainage may be a problem, put down a three-inch base of gravel, top that with an inch or two of peat moss, then add a layer of rich soil and compost that will bring the site back to grade. Pull soil up around the outer sides, for improved insulation.

*TEMPERATURE:* The danger of heat and dehydration is far greater than the danger of cold, even during the early spring and late fall when you will be using your cold frame the most. Remember that even on the coldest winter day, the bright sun can quickly push the temperature in the cold frame up to above 75 or 80 degrees, which should be the maximum. Provide a system of props so that, if there is a chance of overheating, the sash can be raised. Unless prevailing winds blow directly into the cold frame, there is little danger of damaging plants through chilling them.

Here's an excellent compromise between a cold frame and a hotbed. It's a cold frame that uses a cellar wall and window for its back wall. On cold nights, the frame can be covered, and the cellar window left open, and there's no danger of frost, with little expense for heat from the cellar. If the window is large enough, it's even possible to work out of it and into the cold frame area, so that work can be done when it is dark or uncomfortably cold outside. The wall and window, of course, should face south for maximum efficiency.

*USE OF COLD FRAME:* In the spring, when the cold frame will get its greatest use, there are several methods to experiment with. One is to plant hardy vegetables and flowers directly in the cold frame soil. This can be done with cabbages and their relatives, lettuce, and other hardy types. Another method is to seed these into flats, then place the flats in the cold frames. And yet another is used with heat-loving plants such as tomatoes, peppers and eggplants. These can be started under lights indoors or in a hotbed, then transplanted into peatpots and later transferred to the cold frame for hardening off before going into the garden. A beauty of the cold frame is its adaptability to the gardening habits of everyone.

When seeding directly into the cold frame soil, make rows only an inch or two apart, thin ruthlessly, and move plants out and into the garden before they are competing for sunlight and growing room and becoming weakened in the process.

If plants such as tomatoes in peatpots are moved to the cold frame, it is good to cushion them on a blanket of compost or peat moss, well dampened. They will quickly push roots out through the sides of the pots and into the moss, providing an even stronger network of roots when moved into the garden.

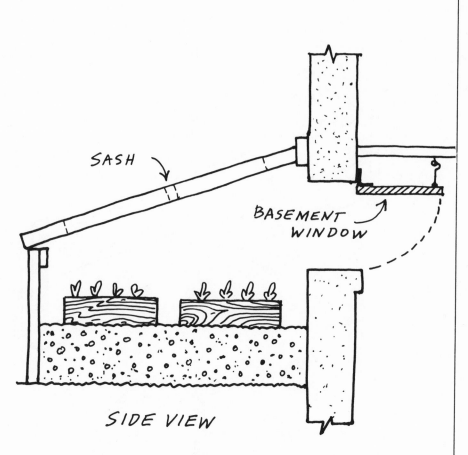

SASH

BASEMENT WINDOW

SIDE VIEW

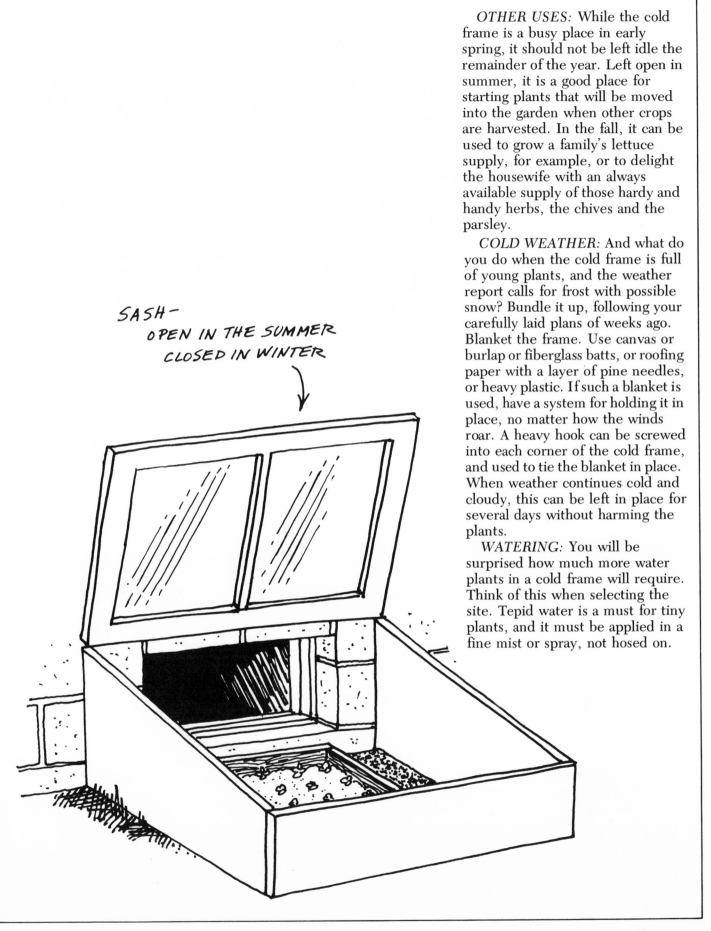

SASH—
OPEN IN THE SUMMER
CLOSED IN WINTER

*OTHER USES:* While the cold frame is a busy place in early spring, it should not be left idle the remainder of the year. Left open in summer, it is a good place for starting plants that will be moved into the garden when other crops are harvested. In the fall, it can be used to grow a family's lettuce supply, for example, or to delight the housewife with an always available supply of those hardy and handy herbs, the chives and the parsley.

*COLD WEATHER:* And what do you do when the cold frame is full of young plants, and the weather report calls for frost with possible snow? Bundle it up, following your carefully laid plans of weeks ago. Blanket the frame. Use canvas or burlap or fiberglass batts, or roofing paper with a layer of pine needles, or heavy plastic. If such a blanket is used, have a system for holding it in place, no matter how the winds roar. A heavy hook can be screwed into each corner of the cold frame, and used to tie the blanket in place. When weather continues cold and cloudy, this can be left in place for several days without harming the plants.

*WATERING:* You will be surprised how much more water plants in a cold frame will require. Think of this when selecting the site. Tepid water is a must for tiny plants, and it must be applied in a fine mist or spray, not hosed on.

# Hotbeds

The cold frame, developed centuries ago, could be called a solar-heated device to give it a modern touch. Add any other source of heat and you have a hotbed.

The original way to provide heat was to put a deep layer of fermenting manure under the soil. With electricity much more expensive today, the person with an available supply of horse, cow or chicken manure might consider trying it.

For a 3'x6' bed, a cubic yard of fresh manure, with one-third of it straw or other litter, is needed.

Pile it 10-12 days in advance and dampen it if it is dry. In 4-5 days it should be heating. Turn pile, getting outer materials into center where they will also heat up. In 4-5 more days it should be ready.

IN WINTER MOUND SOIL OR SAWDUST AGAINST FRAME

SOIL 6"

MANURE 18"

SIDE VIEW OF ORGANIC HOTBED

Dig two feet down on the hotbed site and remove all soil. The sides of the hotbed should be built wide enough to fit to the bottom of this excavation. Put hotbed into place, then shovel in 8″ of manure, building it in layers which should be packed down. On top of this place the soil, 6″ deep if you plan to plant directly into it, 2″ if containers will be placed on it. Manure should continue to generate heat for at least two weeks.

Control of temperature is difficult since there is no relationship between the heat desired and the heat generated.

Here are two sketches of manure-heated beds. The larger one, with the 22″ bed of manure, is six feet square, and, for easy use, has two 3′x6′ sashes on top. Most builders acquire sashes or old storm windows, then fit the beds to the dimensions of those windows.

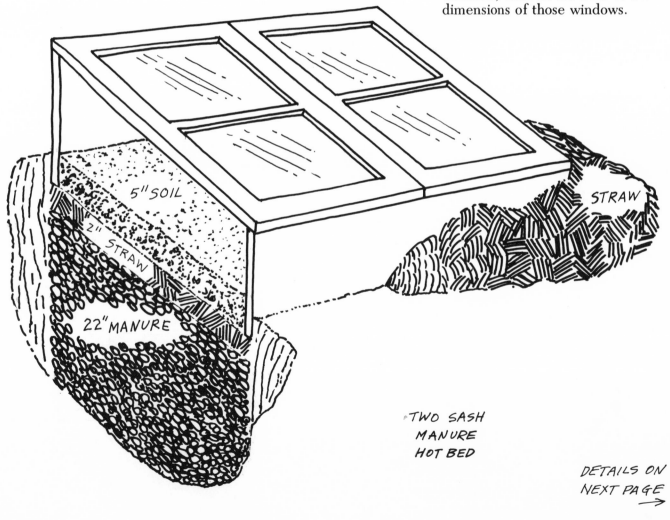

5″ SOIL

2″ STRAW

22″ MANURE

STRAW

TWO SASH MANURE HOT BED

DETAILS ON NEXT PAGE →

Other sources of heat are electricity, from light bulbs or thermostatically controlled electric cable, and in elaborate hotbeds, from hot water pipes and steam.

For the beginner, we recommend the lead-covered electric cable which is thermostatically controlled, thus promising constant temperature and a saving of electricity. The 60-foot cable length should be adequate for the 3′x6′ bed, but this should be checked against the recommendations of manufacturers of specific cables.

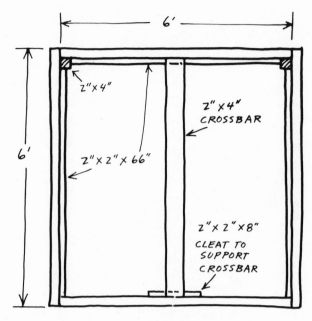

PLAN
(FOR TWO-SASH FRAME)

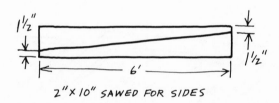

2″X10″ SAWED FOR SIDES

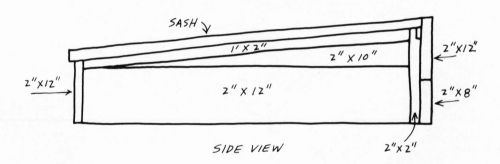

SIDE VIEW

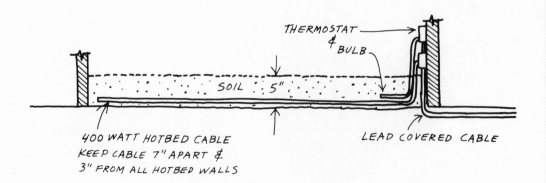

400 WATT HOTBED CABLE
KEEP CABLE 7″ APART &
3″ FROM ALL HOTBED WALLS

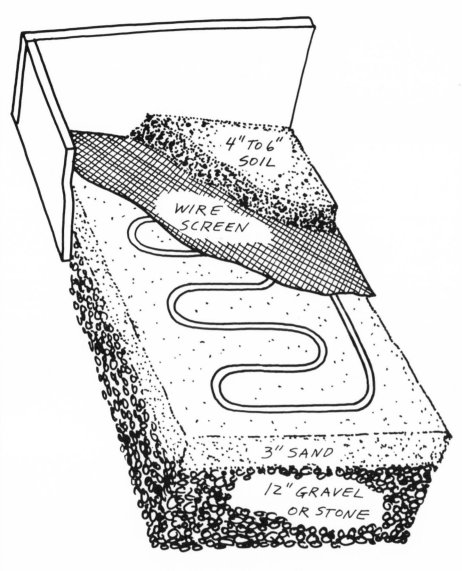

4" TO 6"
SOIL

WIRE
SCREEN

3" SAND

12" GRAVEL
OR STONE

SIDE VIEW
OF
ELECTRIC
HOT BED

Careful installation will result in heat saving and lower electricity costs, and thus more satisfactory operation. Excavate about 20″ of soil from the site, and build sides of hotbed to reach down to this level, for insulation. To assure proper drainage put down a foot-deep layer of crushed gravel. Top this with two or three inches of sand or vermiculite for a bed for the cable. Now loop the cable along the bed, keeping it about two inches from the edges, and making certain it does not cross over on itself. On top of this place a sheet of either hardware cloth or wire screen with a fine mesh. This will assist in spreading the heat evenly in the bed. Then add four to six inches of soil.

This bed is valuable for starting all flowers and vegetables, and is particularly good for starting the heat-loving plants such as tomatoes, eggplants and peppers.

The beginner must watch either the cold frame or hotbed carefully at first since this is when his plants are the most vulnerable.

The chief dangers are overheating, drying out and damping off. The overheating can happen so quickly on a sunny day that operation of these beds is not advised unless there is someone at home all day. The sash must be raised to permit escape of heat. The beds may have to be watered more than once daily with tepid water to maintain an adequate water supply. At the same time, if the air and soil are too damp and the air is warm and humid, conditions are ideal for spreading of the fungus disease known as damping-off. Again, this condition can be corrected by opening the sash to provide fresh air.

Conservation of heat will mean lower power expenses for this unit. Thus it is good to blanket the glass each night, to minimize the loss of heat through the glass.

# Soil Sifters

A joy of gardening is to work with screened compost when starting tiny plants or transplanting or giving houseplants new soil in which to grow. But screening can be a nuisance unless the gardener has the proper equipment. Here are three sizes. The small ones are fine for the small garden, but its use would be tiring if much compost is to be screened. The larger one on page 86 was designed by Doug Merrilees of Northfield, Vt.

The sifter shown on a garden cart is ideal for garden use, because the screened compost is right there in the cart, ready for transport, as soon as it has found its way through the mesh. Compost is shoveled against the ½-inch wire mesh, and the rejected material falls to the ground, to be shoveled back onto the compost pile.

All will have longer lives if wood in them is treated with wood preservative before they are assembled. And to hold these together firmly, the use of carpenter's glue is recommended.

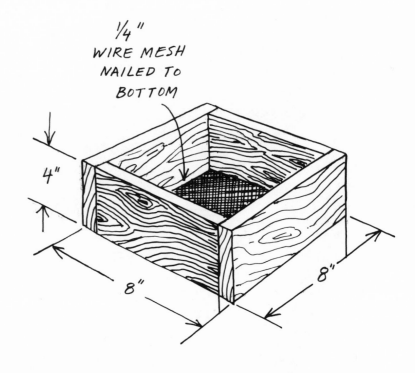

¼" WIRE MESH NAILED TO BOTTOM

4"

8"

8"

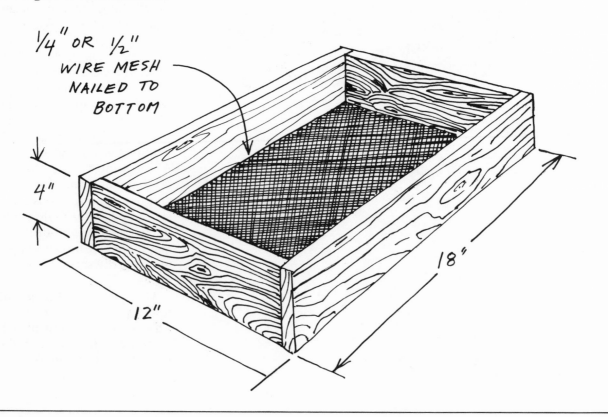

¼" OR ½" WIRE MESH NAILED TO BOTTOM

4"

12"

18"

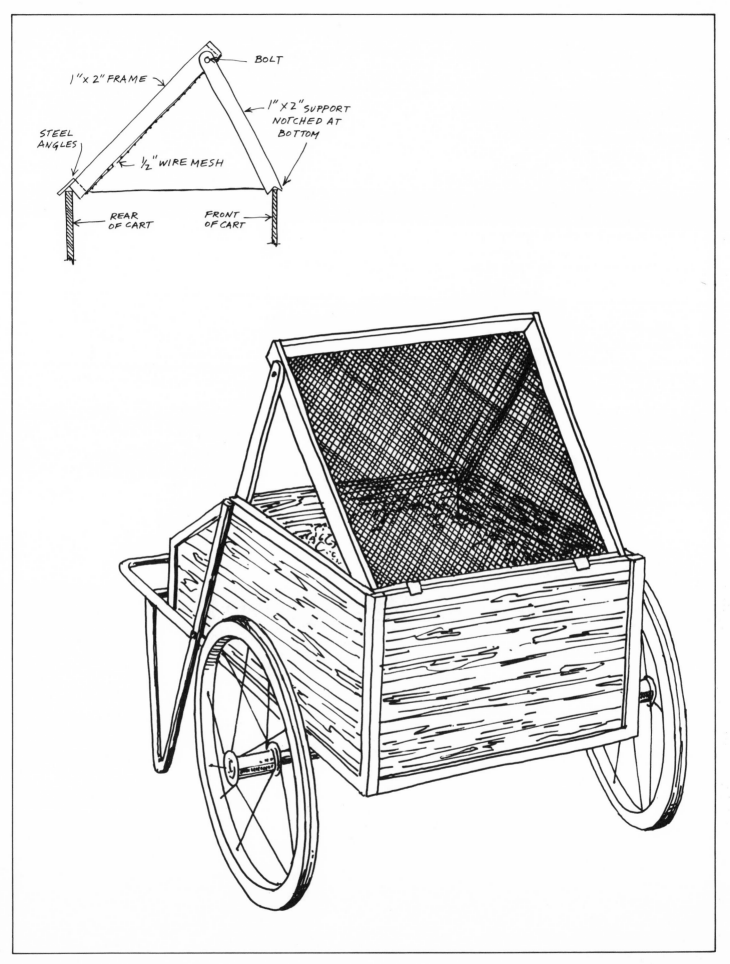

BOLT

1"x 2" FRAME

1" X 2" SUPPORT
NOTCHED AT
BOTTOM

STEEL
ANGLES

½" WIRE MESH

REAR
OF CART

FRONT
OF CART

# Large Sifter

The frame below is made from 1"x6" lumber, two pieces 60" long and two pieces 28½". Nail and glue all corners. The bottom is a piece of ⅜" wire mesh firmly stapled on.

Nail and glue on the two reinforcing blocks to each side of the frame. Drill ½"D holes to fit the ¼"x3" bolt tightly.

The stand is made of the same size lumber, using two 30" pieces and two 31¾" pieces. Nail and glue all joints, adding the corner blocks which are cut from a section of 2"x2". Drill 9/32"D holes three inches from the top.

Give each part two coats of wood preservative before assembling.

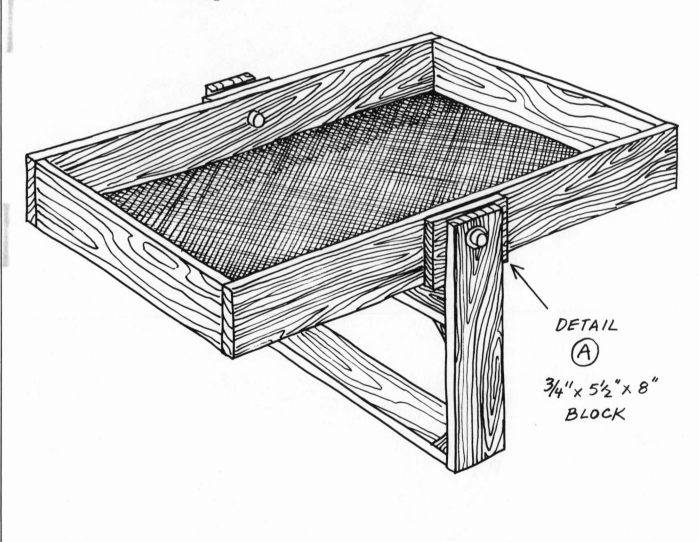

DETAIL
Ⓐ
¾"x 5½"x 8"
BLOCK

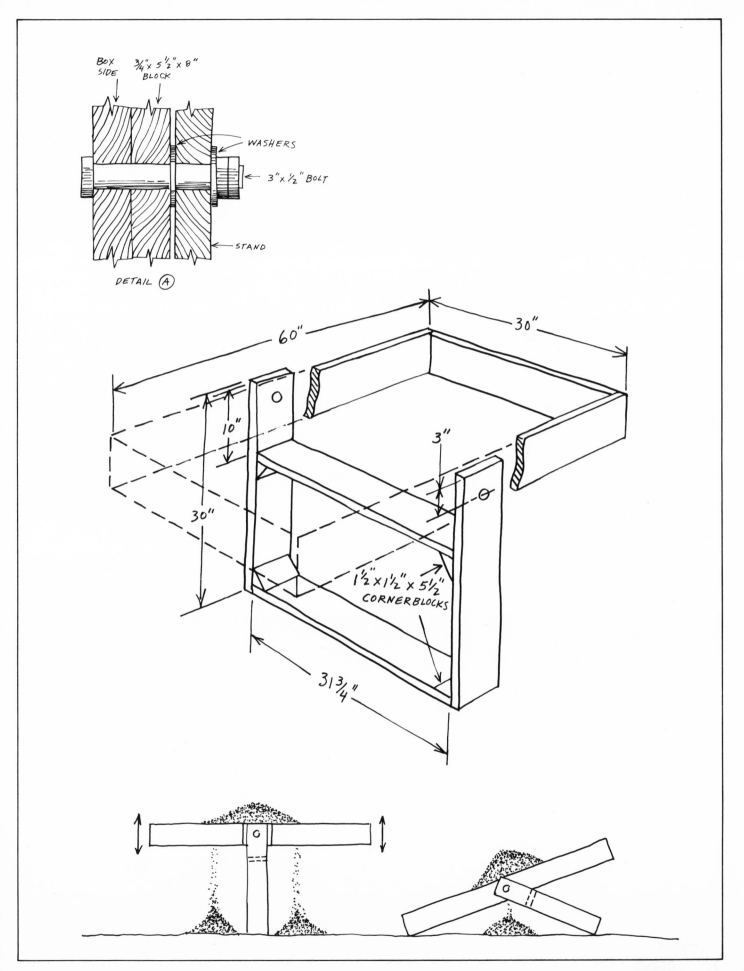

BOX SIDE

$3/4" \times 5\frac{1}{2}" \times 8"$ BLOCK

WASHERS

$3" \times \frac{1}{2}"$ BOLT

STAND

DETAIL Ⓐ

60"

30"

10"

3"

30"

$1\frac{1}{2}" \times 1\frac{1}{2}" \times 5\frac{1}{2}"$ CORNERBLOCKS

$31\frac{3}{4}"$

# Seedling Containers

The list of containers that can be used for seed-starting is a long one. Here are just a few suggestions. There are many more. The ideal ones have certain things in common. They are 2½-3 inches deep, so that the little seedlings can put down relatively long roots, and the soil will not dry out quickly. And they have holes in the bottom, or holes can be punched in them, so the roots are not drowned by overenthusiastic watering, and so "bottom watering," the preferred method for seedlings, is possible.

But for true convenience and long-lasting use, build some flats. This one, a typical size, is 12 by 18 by 2¾ inches. Small space for drainage is left between bottom boards, and a single layer of newspaper is placed in flat before it is filled with soil. This size is easy to handle, deep enough for root growth, and is easily used with peat pots or plant bands for plants which dislike the rigors of transplanting. Can you use scrap lumber to build these? Of course.

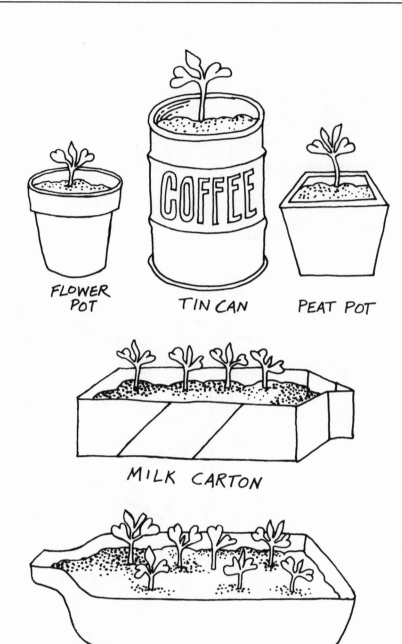

FLOWER POT

TIN CAN

PEAT POT

MILK CARTON

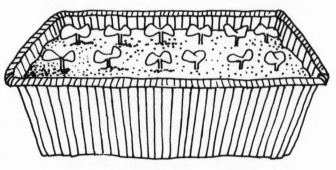

HALF OF ONE-GALLON PLASTIC JUG

FRUIT CARTON

ALUMINUM FOIL PAN

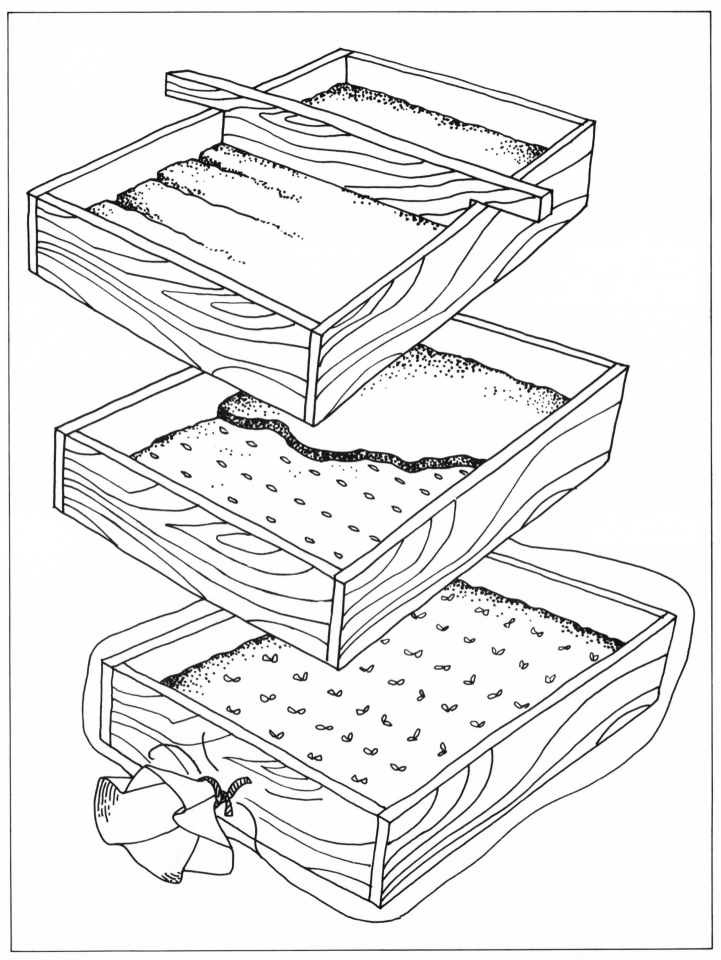

# Plant Protectors

Those birds and animals that feast on your just-up seedlings can be discouraged, and here's the way they do it. Use small mesh wire fabric and plant seeds in trenches so the seedlings can be bridged with 12″ strips. Fill in trench gradually as plants grow. Or bend wire fabric edges about 2″ and bridge planted seed.

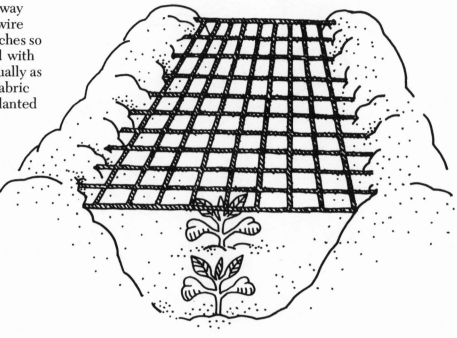

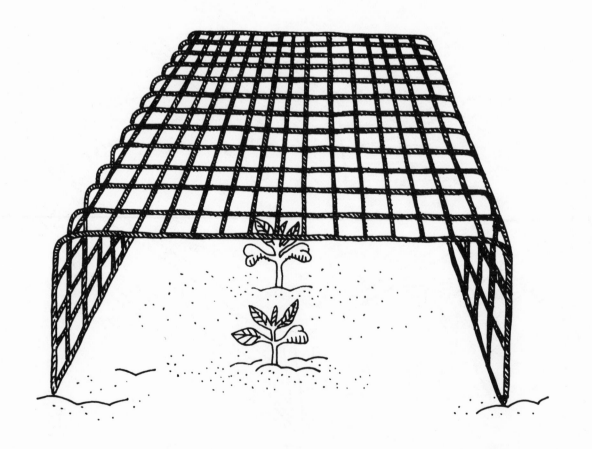

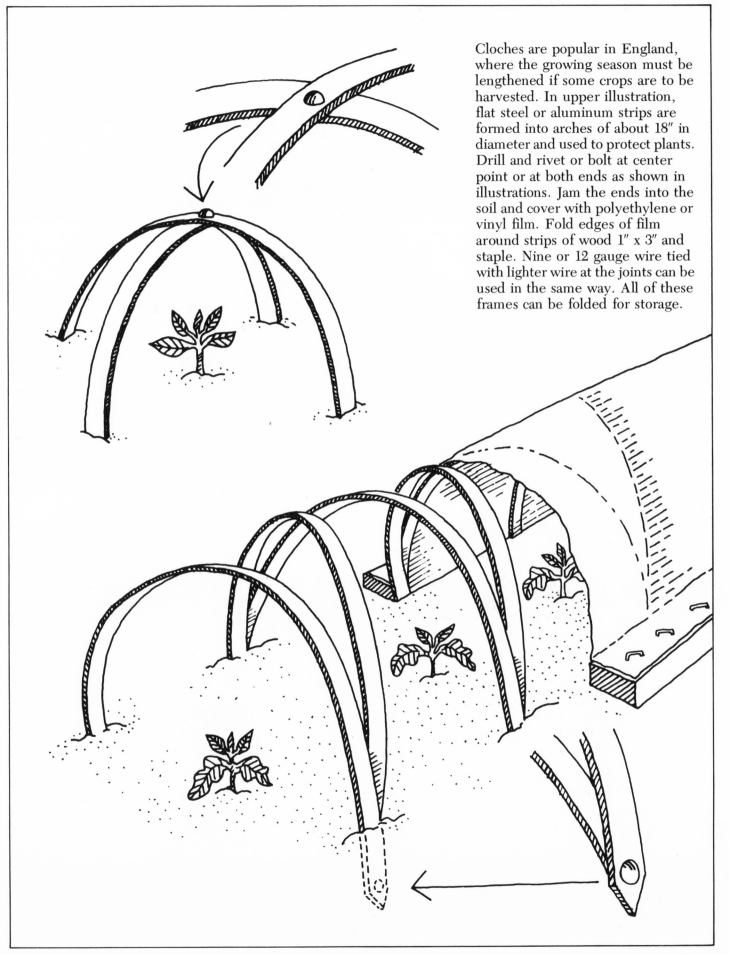

Cloches are popular in England, where the growing season must be lengthened if some crops are to be harvested. In upper illustration, flat steel or aluminum strips are formed into arches of about 18″ in diameter and used to protect plants. Drill and rivet or bolt at center point or at both ends as shown in illustrations. Jam the ends into the soil and cover with polyethylene or vinyl film. Fold edges of film around strips of wood 1″ x 3″ and staple. Nine or 12 gauge wire tied with lighter wire at the joints can be used in the same way. All of these frames can be folded for storage.

Mesh reinforced plastic, often used as a substitute for window glass, has a place in the garden. Here are three ways it can be used to protect plants from animals as well as the elements. Illustration at left shows it is stiff enough so that it can be formed into arches by stapling the edges to strips of wood. Soil tamped into place will hold the arch. Cones and cylinders are good for individual plants, arch for tiny plants in a row.

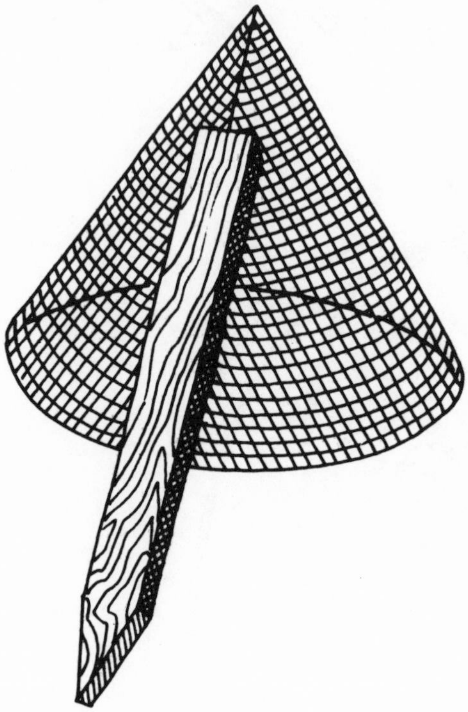

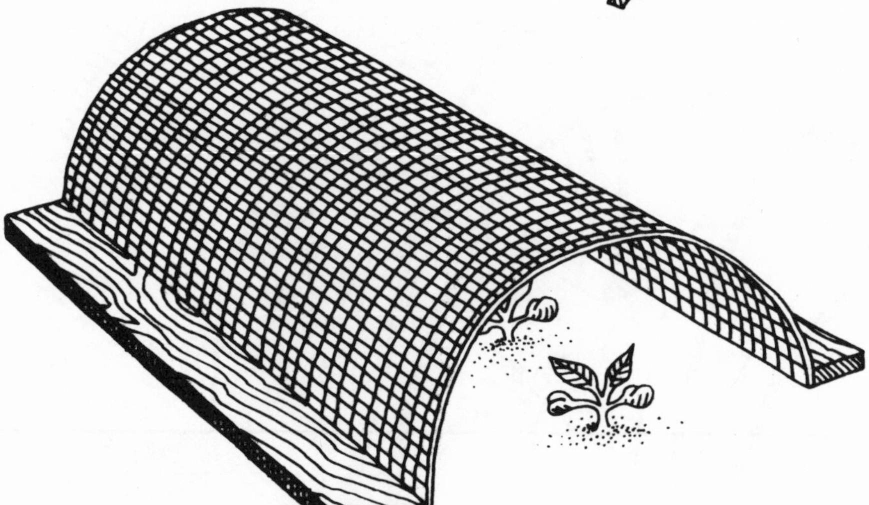

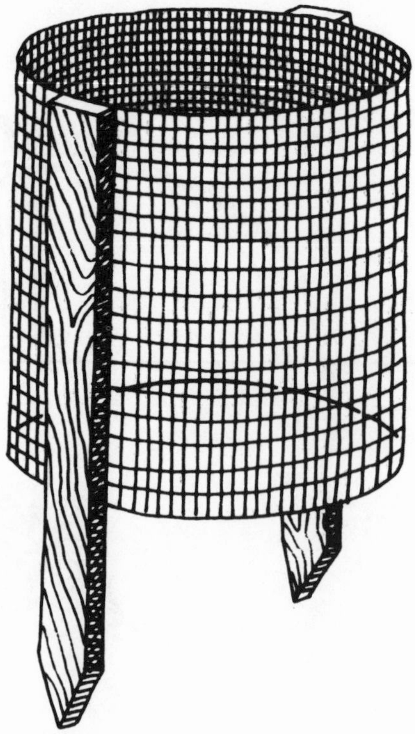

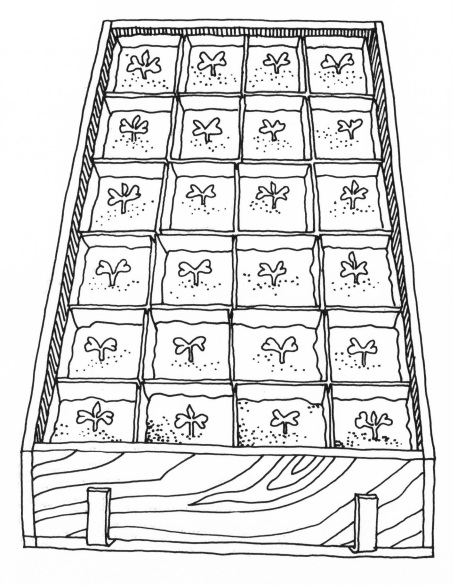

## Planting Tray

Here's something for nothing that will help you in starting your garden produce in the spring. Each of these planting trays that you build will save you the cost of 24 peat pots, and work fully as well.

You'll need a quantity of quart milk cartons, washed and drained after being emptied of their milk. (They're smelly if unwashed.)

You'll also need some light scrap lumber. If it includes a few pieces of exterior plywood, fine.

Cut tops and bottoms off milk cartons. This leaves you with square boxes, 7½" tall and 2¾" square. Cut each of these twice, so that each produces three boxes, 2½" tall.

Place 24 of these boxes side by side so they form a rectangle of six by four boxes. This is the shape that you want for your planting tray. The interior dimensions of boxes that I build are 16½" by 11". Use a piece of exterior plywood as a bottom, and scrap lumber sides 3" high. That's all there is to it—unless you think ahead, and if you do you will wonder how you are going to lift the first plant out of that box without injuring it or others. It will be difficult.

So, make the plywood base of the box an inch longer, and make two facing side pieces an inch longer too. Then nail a cleat at the inside edge of each of those two side pieces. Thus the fourth side will not be nailed in place, but will be held there between the cleats and the planting bands. It can be easily slipped out at transplanting time, and the individual plants slipped out without damage.

I have used these for starting all members of the brassica or cabbage family, such as cauliflower, cabbage and broccoli. I place the bands in the box, fill them with a rich soil mixture, then transplant seedlings into them from flats. They're useful for many other vegetables too, and flowers.

# Garden Layout Stakes

Spend 15 minutes now, and save hours later. That's the story of garden layout stakes like these. Once built, and it's a job that can be done in minutes, they will last for years, and save you those annual hunts for stakes. Built like those in the illustration, they will insure that your planting rows are evenly spaced and parallel. Four-foot lengths of any 1"x3" wood will do providing they are sound and fairly straight. They should project enough beyond the lower peg to be pointed and to stand up in soft earth. (Six inches, at least.)

The row width is shown as three feet. Vary this to suit your own preference. The pegs are 6-inch lengths of ½-inch dowel. Drill all the way through the wood and glue these in place with waterproof glue. Use two coats of wood preservative or paint and tie enough twine to extend the full width of your garden.

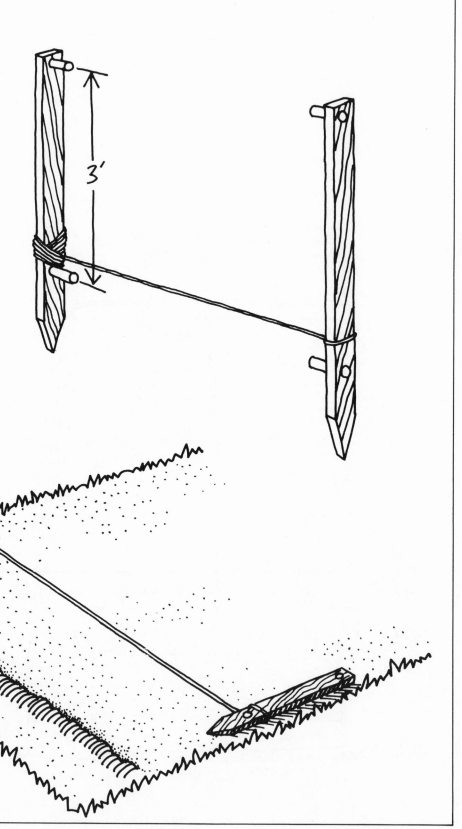

# Berry Box

Berry pickers, here's a way to prevent crushing those fragile raspberries. A way to know exactly how many strawberries you have picked. And you'll find this useful around the garden too, when picking other small produce.

This berry box carrier, built to hold six quart cartons, is the brainchild of Louise Riotte, who wrote *The Complete Guide to Growing Berries and Grapes*.

Louise says to use scrap lumber for this. Make it of light lumber, since you'll be carrying it a lot—and full of berries, too, we hope. Make a shallow box, 11″ by 16½″ by 2½″ deep. Attach two 19″-long pieces of 1″x2″ on either side, and bring them together at the top, nailing them to a short section of broomstick or a 20″ piece of 1″x2″ for a handle.

Another berrying tip from Louise: Leave the caps on your strawberries for they impart a special sweetness and should not be removed until you are ready to use them. Refrigerate berries for an hour or more, remove, cap and wash in cold water to which you have added a few ice cubes. Drain on paper towels.

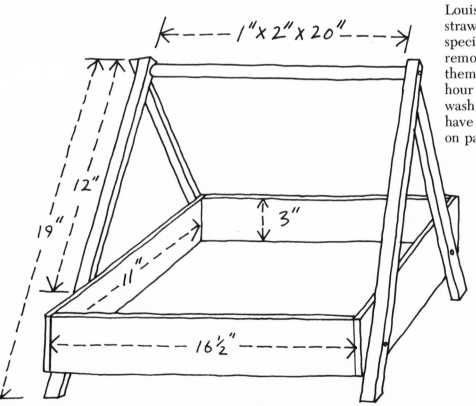

DISCARDED BROOM HANDLES ARE STRONG AND EASY TO CARRY BOX BY

# Strawberry Pyramid

If you have a spot where a strawberry pyramid can be featured, try it, using one of the two methods shown here.

Many add a fountain effect to their pyramids by installing a sprinkler head in the top center. This of course can be attached to a plastic hose, buried under the pyramid and leading to a source of water.

A common commercial model that can be purchased complete with sprinkler and various coverings can be duplicated by the homeowner. Purchase thirty-eight feet of foot-wide aluminum lawn border. This will provide nineteen feet for the base circle, thirteen feet for the second circle, and six feet for the top. Bury the aluminum strips about three inches into the soil. Place the first circle in position, fill it with soil; put the second in position, fill it with soil, then place and fill the third circle. This takes a surprisingly large amount of topsoil. This size will require about one cubic yard, but will provide space for fifty strawberry plants.

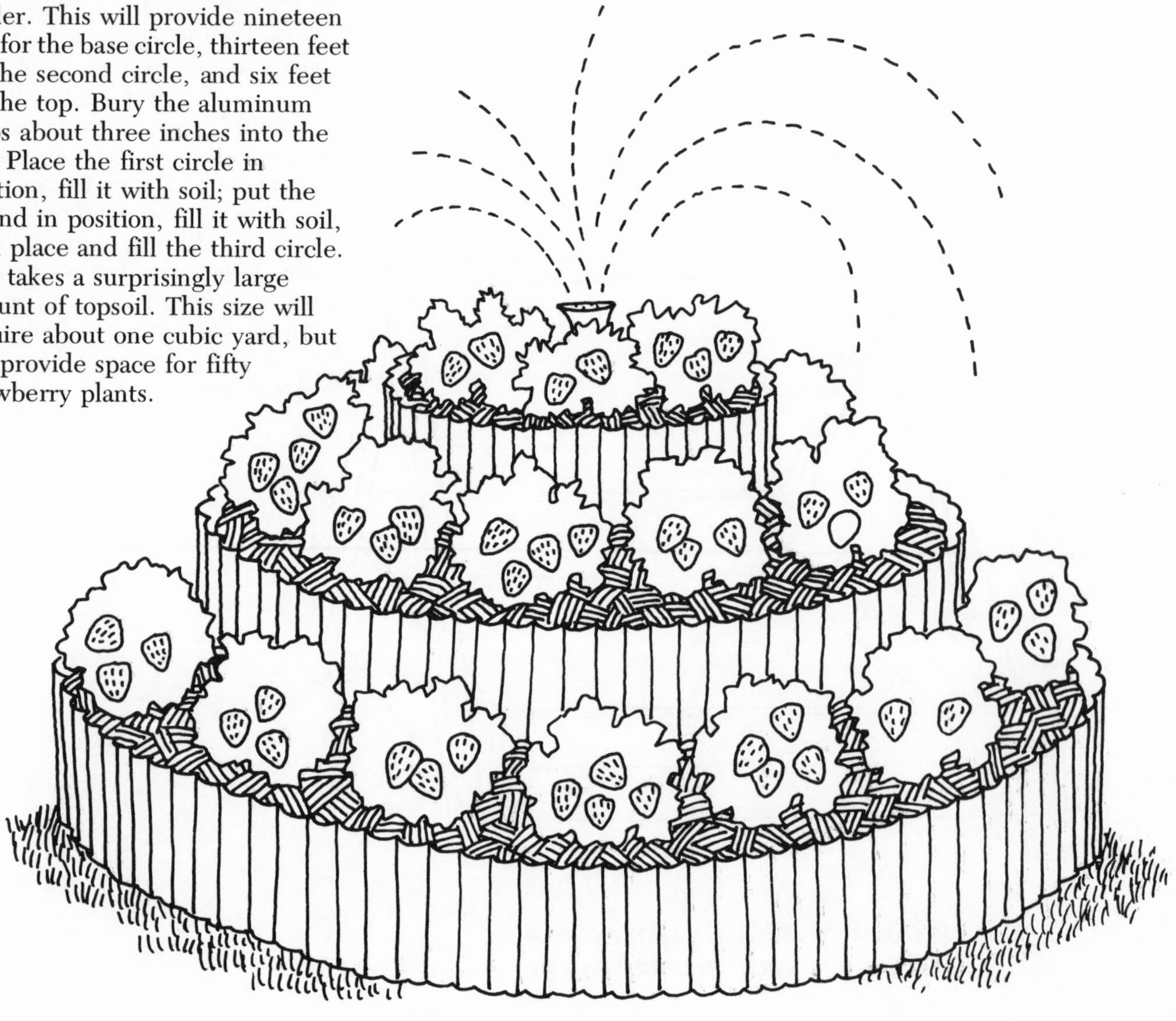

A square bed may be made of lumber treated with a preservative. Squares of sixty inches, thirty-six inches and twelve inches are recommended. If the squares are too large, the gardener will have difficulty working in the beds. Lumber 1"x12" is recommended. Use 24" stakes at two corners of each box to hold the squares in position.

By setting out the plants one year, harvesting the next year, and carefully removing old plants after each harvest, filling their space with the runners that will develop, this bed can be kept in operation for five or six years. Remember, the temptation to be fought is overcrowding of plants. Such over-density of foliage will produce smaller berries. Mulching is particularly desirable, since it will conserve moisture, lower the temperatures around the roots, and keep the berries clean. Pine needles will work fine, and their appearance is pleasant.

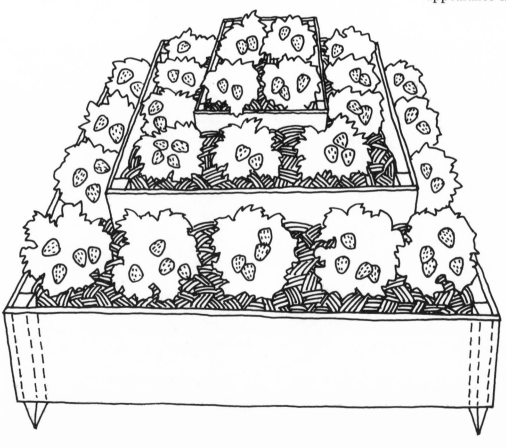

# Strawberry Barrel

A strawberry barrel provides both beauty and berries. If you're going to try one, plan ahead. You'll need a barrel, of course, a rich soil mixture, several shovelsful of sand, a pail of gravel, a piece of window screening, 18″ wide and as long as the barrel is high, several blocks to place under the barrel, and tools to cut the holes—all of these assembled where the barrel will be placed. And strawberry plants.

Bore drainage holes in the bottom of the barrel. Then in a row 8″ from the bottom and 8″ apart, cut holes for the plants. An easy way to cut these is to bore a triangle of holes 2″ apart, then cut out the resulting triangle with a coping saw. Stagger similar rows of holes up side of barrel, with holes never closer than 8″ apart.

Put 3″-4″ of gravel or small stones in bottom of barrel, for drainage. Roll window screening into long tube and tie into shape with wire. Place tube in center of barrel where, when it is filled with sand, it will serve as a funnel to get water to soil at all levels.

Rich soil is needed. One formula is to mix one part each of sand, topsoil and compost, adding one shovelful each of rotted manure and bone meal to each bushel of mixture.

Begin putting soil mixture into barrel, sand into tube, until both reach half-way up first row of triangles. Plant each strawberry plant along the side of the barrel, with crown of plant and foliage protruding out of hole. Water, making certain crown and plant don't settle below level of hole in barrel. Fill barrel to next level of holes and repeat process. When barrel is filled, plant a few plants 8″ apart on top.

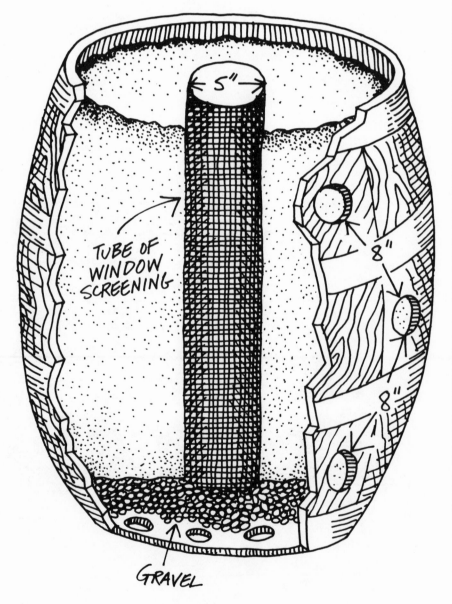

TUBE OF WINDOW SCREENING

GRAVEL

Barrel should be shifted a quarter-turn counterclockwise every few days to balance light on plants. Like all strawberry plants, these should not be allowed to produce fruit the first year. Keep blossoms picked, so growth will go into plants. Don't let plants produce runners, either, unless a few are needed to replace dead plants in barrel.

After first heavy frost, move barrel into garage or barn, or wrap it in a blanket of straw or hay, to protect plants.

This type of barrel has other uses, such as for sedums, and can be particularly attractive planted with a variety of the smaller herbs, such as basil and creeping thyme.

# Massive Pots

If you need massive pots for outdoor planting, and the prices of them are discouraging you, visit your home construction store and see the various sizes of terra cotta flue tiles he has. Set in place, and with a small piece of plastic underneath to prevent plant roots from extending down into the soil, they make dramatic plant holders. A drawback is that they may be more difficult to move than conventional pots, since soil will drop out of bottom unless they are handled very carefully. A strong point is that drainage in them is excellent. No plants will drown in them, as in pots without holes in their bottoms.

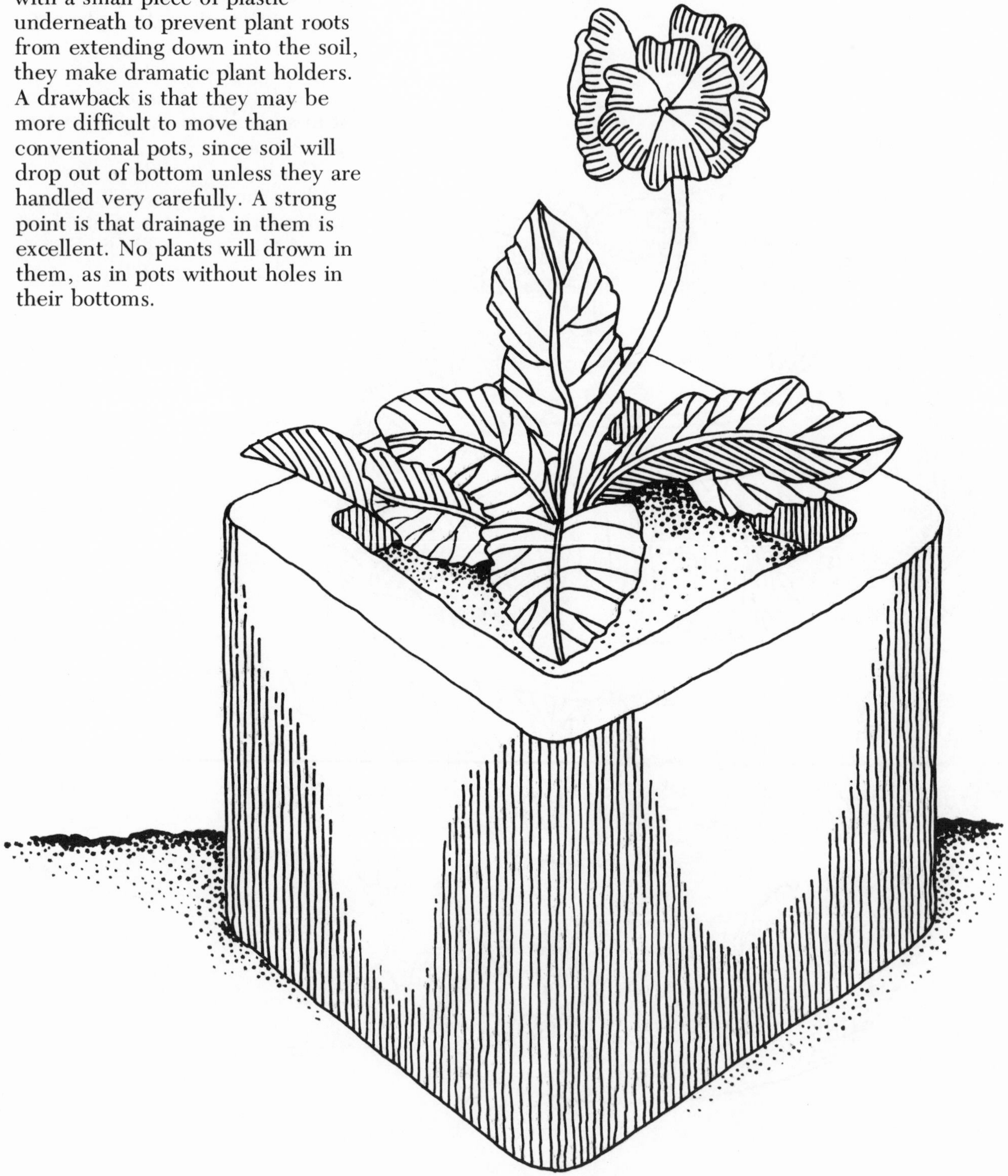

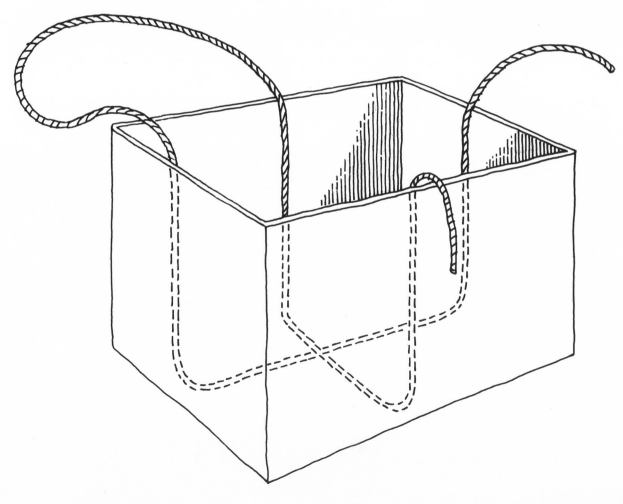

## Baling Hay

Fred Ormsby's problem was a delightful one. A neighbor of his had the hay cut on a small lot and, knowing Fred's love of hay for mulch, offered him the hay if he would pick it up. The problem: How to store it? Best solution, and an expensive one, would have been to have a hay baler do the job. Fred decided to do it himself. His tools were a sturdy cardboard carton, a ball of baling twine, and children eager to help. Fred would place the baling twine in the box, from front to back, looped over to one side, then back across the box again. The children gathered and stomped the hay into the box and Fred tied it. Result: Bales of hay enough to cover the strawberries in the fall, and some saved for use the following spring.

# Plant Supports

Most plants benefit one way or another by being supported. Keeping tomatoes, squash, and other fleshy vegetables off the ground reduces the possibility of mold and rot caused by dampness or fungus in the earth. With the stalks and leaves off the ground, mulch is easily applied to the ground below. By training plants to grow upright, considerable space is conserved, and with land becoming scarcer and gardens by necessity having to be smaller, more can be grown on a smaller piece of land.

*MATERIALS.* Most of these aids can be made of scrap wood or of low grade lumber which need not be kiln dried, and other materials easily available from your local hardware store or lumber dealer.

*WOOD.* Almost any species of wood is suitable for gardening aids. Soft wood is more easily worked, and when ordering from a lumber yard you will get any of a number of species unless you specify a particular one. These would include pine, hemlock, spruce, larch, and fir. The heartwood of cypress, cedar and redwood is resistant to decay and will cost more.

For gardening purposes the grade of lumber labeled "No. 3 common" is adequate. Wood can be ordered by the board foot (a board foot is the equivalent of 12″ by 12″ by 1″ thick) or by linear feet. It is more convenient to estimate the number of linear feet in the size you want for a particular job (forty-eight feet of 1″x3″) and to order this way than to translate into board feet. Remember also that lumber is specified by nominal dimensions at the time of sawing. Subsequent planing reduces these dimensions. Boards are cut to even foot dimensions, six, eight, ten and twelve feet long.

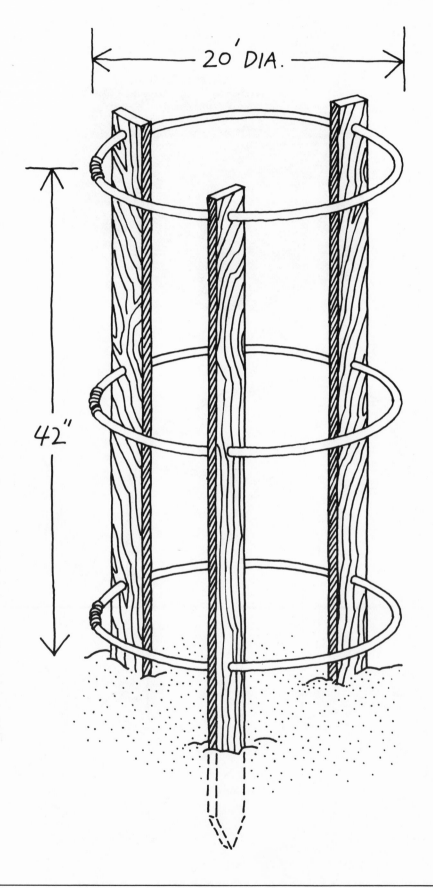

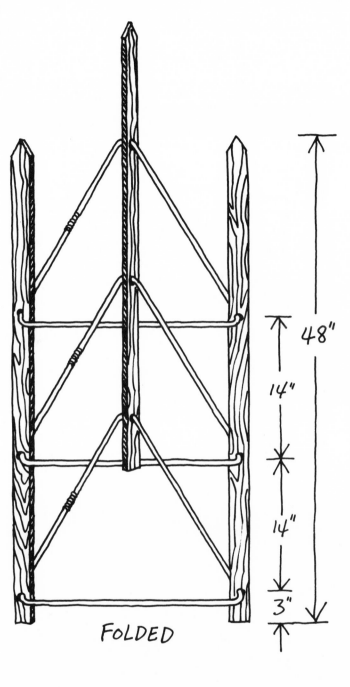

FOLDED

48"

14"

14"

3"

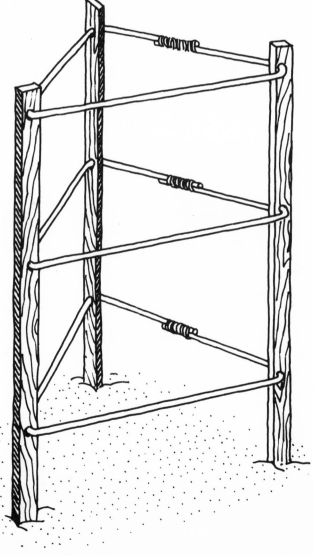

*LATH.* Wood lath measures ⅜″ by one by four feet long and is made of various species. The surfaces are unplaned and it must be handled with care to avoid slivers. Lath is extremely useful around the garden for many purposes.

*WIRE.* Ideally wire should be non-rusting for outdoor uses. However, galvanized iron wire will delay rusting.

*WIRE FABRIC.* A term used for woven wire products. It is made in mesh sizes from ½″ x ½″ up to 4″ x 4″ square mesh and in various widths up to 6 feet wide and in rolls 50 or 100 feet long. Hardware stores and lumber dealers will cut the length you ask for.

*FASTENINGS* should all be non-rusting or galvanized. You will find 6d and 8d nails adequate for most needs. Galvanized wire staples should be used for fastening wire fabric to wood.

*PRESERVATIVES.* Wood will last longer if coated or soaked with wood preservative. Redwood, cypress, cedar and locust have a natural resistance to rot and insect enemies and will last longer than other woods. However, all woods will benefit if treated with a preservative.

Do not use creosote, as it is poisonous to nearby plants. The most widely recommended preservative is pentachlorophenol, popularly known as "penta" and available under a variety of trade names. It is best to soak the whole length of wood for at least 24 hours. At least soak the ends that will come in contact with the earth, using a bucket filled with preservative.

Fresh-cut saplings will not absorb much preservative, none at all if the bark is left on. Saplings should be cut well in advance of the time you intend to use them. The bark should be peeled off and then should be allowed to dry before soaking them.

Many gardeners contend that you can raise more tomatoes if you don't tie them up in any way, just let them run along the ground.

And we agree. You will have more tomatoes. More for the slugs. More to rot. More to step on as you reach out, trying for one far away.

For the best crop, get those vines off the ground.

There are many ways to do it. The most-used system is a stake, pounded deep into the ground for good support, and the tomato plant tied to it with some materials that will not cut into the plant. Strips torn from old sheets work fine. For many plants, six feet of stake above ground is not too much.

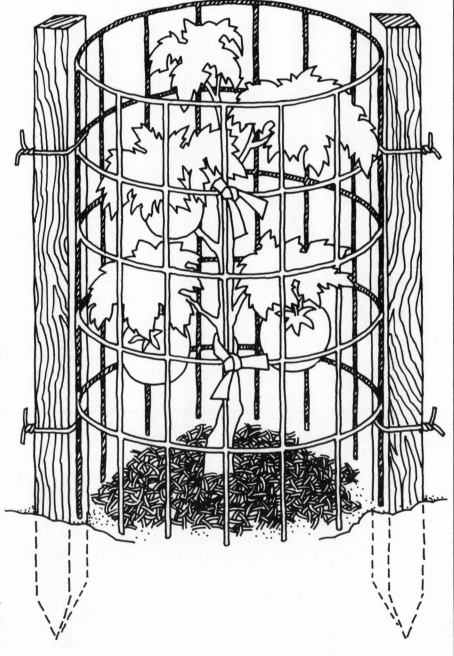

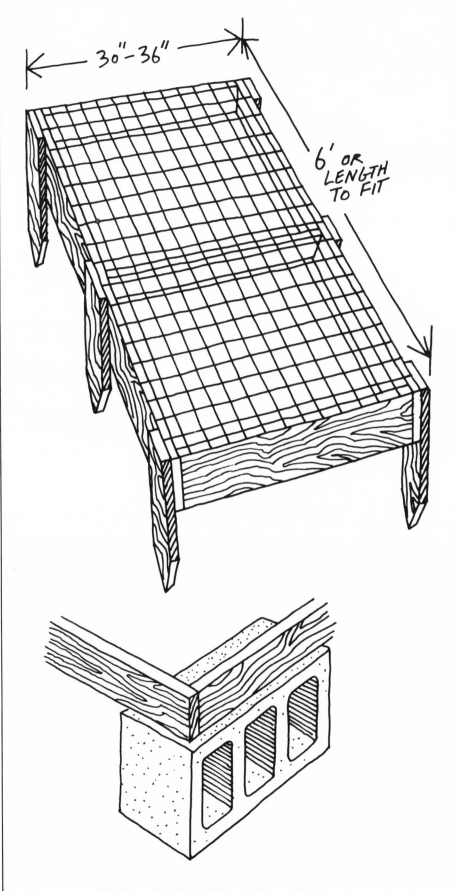

30"–36"

6' OR LENGTH TO FIT

Of the many methods of holding tomatoes that have been tried, we'll go for the tomato cylinder. Concrete reinforcing wire with a six-inch mesh and five feet in width is ideal. Cut a four-foot piece, round it into a cylinder and tie it in shape with wire. Set it over the tomato plant, and hold it there with two stakes. It's easy to train the vines in this cylinder, and picking tomatoes is a joy, particularly if you have struggled with sprawling, earthbound vines before.

Douglas Merrilees recommended shapes such as these to hold tomatoes and other plants. They're easy to make of nine or twelve gauge wire. Rings are about twenty inches in diameter, and triangles are about twenty inches on each side. Slip rings or triangles through holes and bind ends together with lighter wire. The rings or triangles should be the same size, so the unit will fold together neatly for storage. He used lath, and drilled half-inch holes in it for the rings.

Make rings or triangles of 9 or 12 gauge wire. Rings should be about 20″ diameter and triangles 20″ each side. Clamp three pieces of lath together and drill 3 ½″ holes as shown. Slip rings or triangles through holes and bind ends together with lighter wire. Make sure the rings or triangles are the same size, otherwise they will not fold neatly.

Here's a compromise arrangement for tomatoes that keeps them off the ground, yet lets them grow in their natural position, which is vertical. Doug Merrilees designed this using 1″x2″ frames and 1″x2″ mesh wire. The frame is three feet by six feet, and is held eight inches off the ground by stakes or concrete blocks.

# Tomato Supports

If none of these methods pleases you, here are some more for you to consider.

This one involves poles, with heavy cord at six-inch intervals, so the gardener can weave the plant into the cord as the tomato plant grows. Remember, there will be a lot of weight on those big plants, so don't plan more than two plants between each set of poles.

A similar method is to nail or tie thin poles (saplings are fine) between the poles and tie the tomato plants to them.

The gardener should try several of these methods of holding tomato plants off the soil. He or she will soon know which works the best, accomplishing the most with the least amount of work.

# Garden Fences

A fence around a garden, complete with a gate, adds a note of neatness to your spread. And it serves practical purposes too. Cucumbers, peas and other vegetables will grow on it, and it will halt dogs, roving children and whatever wild animals are sharing your produce with you.

If it's to be decorative, you have your choice of many materials, from split rails to—but don't select it—plastic. If it's woodchucks you're trying to keep out, pick four-foot chickenwire, and bury the bottom a few inches, for those woodchucks will try digging underneath. If it's squirrels, use two strands of electric fencing, one near the outer side and a few inches from the ground, the other an inch or two above the top. And if you're trying to stop coons, forget it. They'll find their way into the First National Bank vault if there's sweet corn locked in there.

Putting up a fence is a lot of work but any extra effort you invest pays off in the years ahead, as the fence stands straight and solid. If you use wooden posts, try for cedar ones, then peel them and soak them in preservative to increase their longevity. Get them fence-high plus two feet, so they can be deep and firm in the ground. A 10-foot span between fence posts is a good average. Pick solid posts for the corners, and anchor them well. Do the same for the posts that will support the gate.

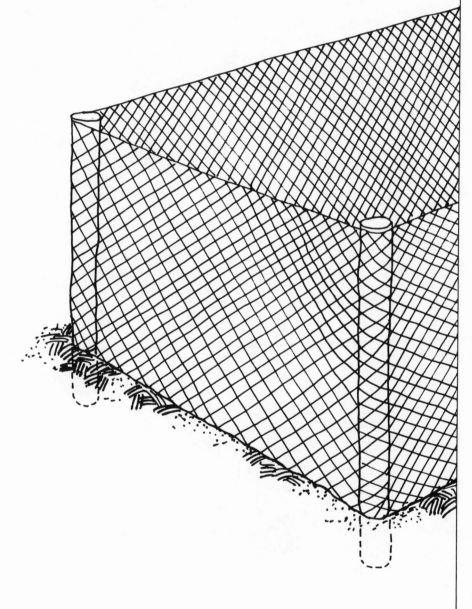

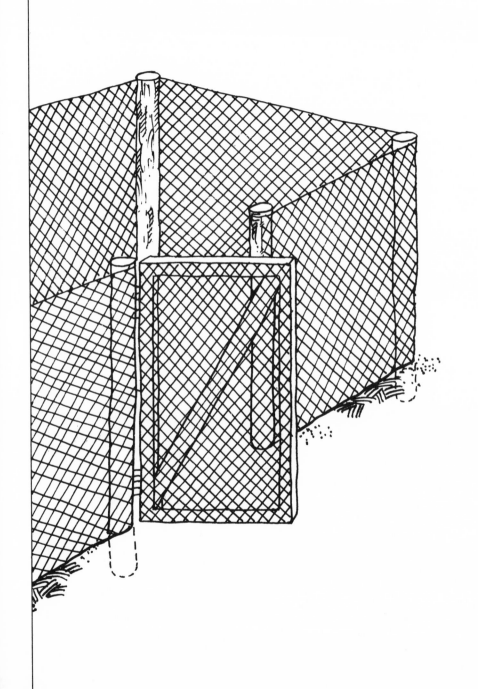

Think before building that gate. What's the largest equipment you will be moving in and out? A wheelbarrow, a tiller or maybe a garden cart? Whichever it is, measure it, and give yourself at least six extra inches of maneuvering room. And plan the best location for that gate. Handy to the path between house and garden. But don't have it lead into the strawberry patch or the asparagus bed. It should lead to a path that provides access to the rest of the garden. A poor location can be an irritating nuisance.

Remember those wild visitors. If you have animal problems, make certain the gate is tight, without squeezing room either on the sides or the bottom. At the bottom, it may be necessary to have the gate swing out of the garden, and, when it is closed, butt against a low rock step.

There's a construction law to obey when building that gate. A rectangle with its four sides is unstable, but a triangle is firm. That's the reason for including a diagonal brace in your design. With a light gate you may get the same stiffness using a wire diagonal tightened with a turnbuckle, such as you may have on your screen door.

Canada Department of Agriculture points out that fence posts will last longer if the tops are cut at an angle and the bases are cut at right angles.

# Setting Posts

When building a fence, or many other structures, it's necessary to set posts in the ground. The simplest method, shown in (A), is to dig a hole, set the post in the ground, then tamp earth around it. If the soil is sandy or unstable, a concrete collar should be poured around the post, after it has been set in the hole and earth tamped around it (B). A temporary brace may be needed to hold the post while the concrete sets.

Posts should be set two feet deep for a five-foot fence, 2½ feet for a six-foot fence, and thirty-six inches is adequate for most eight- to ten-foot structures.

Heartwood of redwood can be used untreated for posts, but other woods should be treated to delay decay.

When putting posts on concrete, post anchors (C) may be used. These are available at building supply dealers. Another method (D) is to imbed a block into the concrete, then nail the post to that. This is less secure than the post anchor. When a concealed anchorage is desired the drift pin (E) may be used. A small space should be left between the bottom of the post and the concrete surface to avoid the accumulation of moisture and dirt.

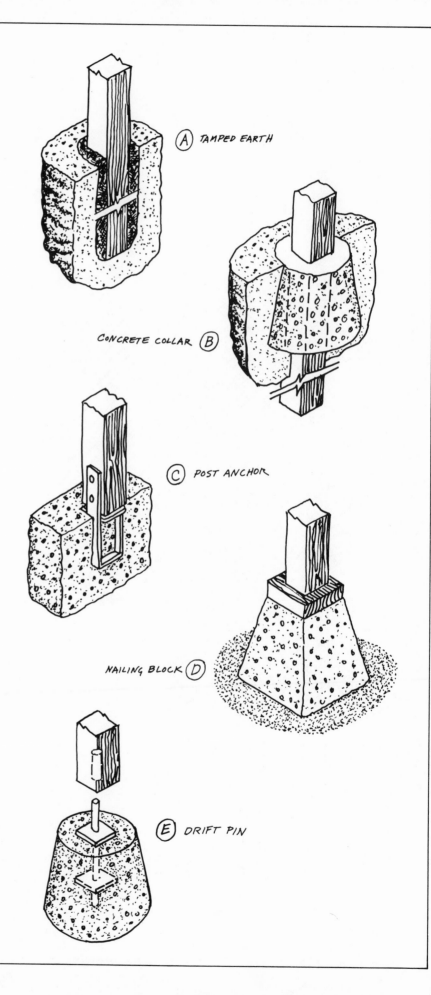

Ⓐ TAMPED EARTH

CONCRETE COLLAR Ⓑ

Ⓒ POST ANCHOR

NAILING BLOCK Ⓓ

Ⓔ DRIFT PIN

# Tight Fence

The graceful lines of loose fencing are not appreciated by fence builders, nor do they strengthen or increase the efficiency of the fence.

The trick is: How to get the fence tight?

If you're building a wooden fence of some kind, there's no problem.

If you're using barbed wire, there are various fence stretchers available. For a garden-size fence, you won't need them. Use a claw hammer or a notched hardwood board to hold the wire while you staple it into place. Dirk van Loon, author of *The Family Cow*, who suggests these two methods, advises the fence-builder to drive the staples at an angle to the wood's grain, to avoid splitting.

A woven fence is more difficult to keep tight. Use of a fence stretcher such as this helps a lot. Note the braced "dummy" post at right.

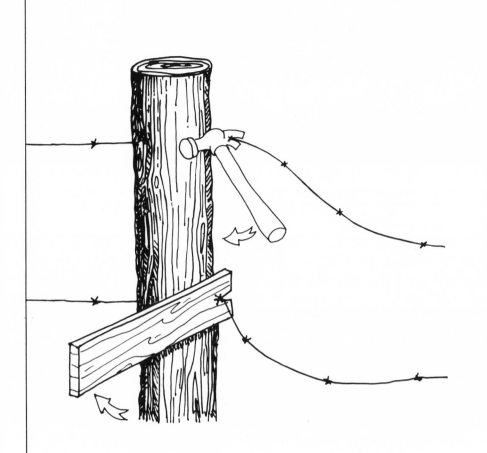

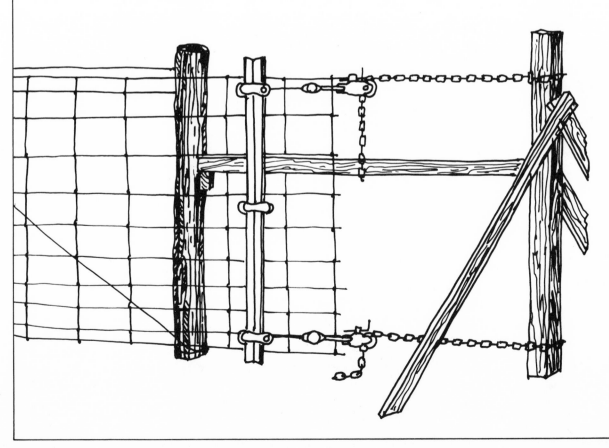

# Corner Posts

The corner posts receive the greatest punishment, and usually are the first to fail. Build them strong, brace them well, and they'll stand the test of the years.

Here are three methods of building a strong corner assembly.

The first one includes a corner post, with two other posts set eight feet away from it, and in line with the fence. Two eight-foot posts span the distance between the corner post and the other two, eight feet away. The corner unit is pulled tightly together by double strands of No. 9 gauge wire, extending from the tops of the two posts to the bottom of the corner post. This wire can be tightened, as shown, by twisting it with a stick.

The same principle is used with the second method, only in this case the lower ends of the wire are sunk into the ground and held by deadmen, which can be rocks or logs. This is a more permanent arrangement.

Finally, for a permanent installation using steel posts, the following is suggested. Note that both the steel corner and the brace posts are set in concrete.

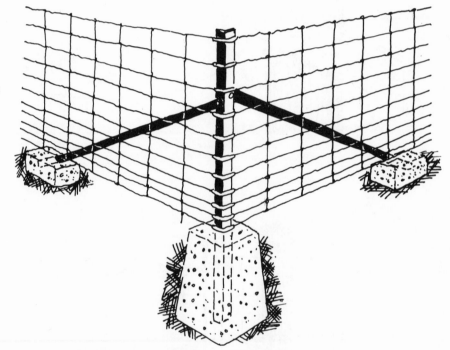

STEEL CORNER & BRACE POSTS
SET IN CONCRETE

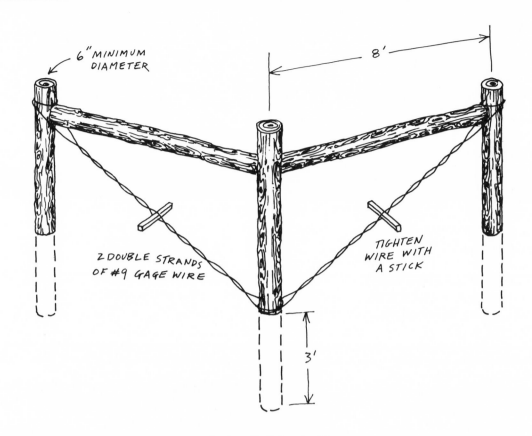

6" MINIMUM DIAMETER

8'

2 DOUBLE STRANDS OF #9 GAGE WIRE

TIGHTEN WIRE WITH A STICK

3'

SINGLE BRACING

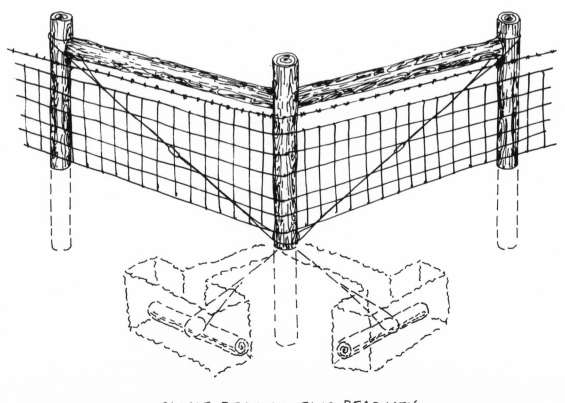

SINGLE BRACING PLUS DEAD MEN

# Electric Fence

Think of the advantages and disadvantages of an electric fence before building one.

Advantages: They're easy and quick to construct, and the materials needed are relatively cheap.

Disadvantages: They're not beautiful; they may shock the neighborhood children causing high tension among families; they require a constant source of electricity; you'll bump into it at least once and be disagreeably reminded of it; they require periodic care in that grass nearby must be kept cut, or the fence will be grounded and ineffective.

Step one in building an electric fence: Check to see whether they are legal in your city, town or county. There's a growing batch of legislation against them, particularly in more settled areas.

What you need for an electric fence depends on what you are fencing in or out. A fence for dairy cattle is often a single strand of wire. Common for a garden is a two-strand fence with one strand about six inches from the ground, and the other three or four feet above it. Often this is used with (and placed outside) a conventional wood or wire fence.

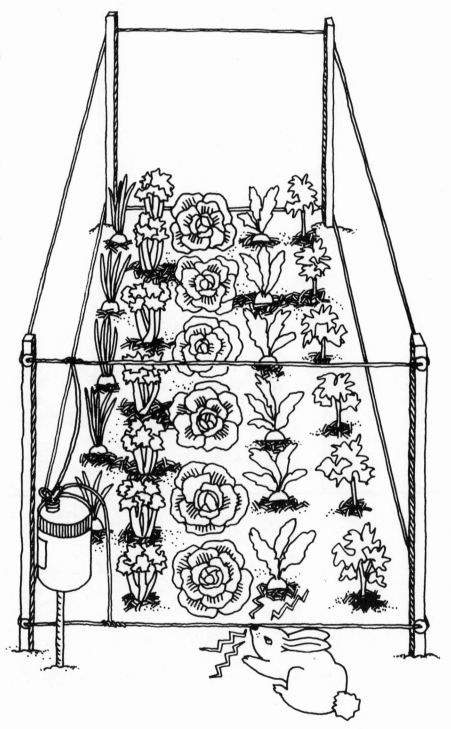

# Preserving Posts

The homesteader who wants to soak large quantities of wood in wood preservative, for pole building construction or for fence posts, will find these suggestions helpful, since a relatively large number can be soaked at one time. For a permanent unit, remove the top and bottom from one 55-gallon drum, the top from another, and weld the first to the top of the second. Coat the inside with roofing tar. Bury the unit to have it at a comfortable working height. Fill with preservative.

The person with only a few posts to soak can build a framework of 2″x4″s or any used lumber. Place this in a hole of suitable length, width and depth, then line the framed hole with heavy plastic sheeting, and fill this tub with the preservative.

For a quick-to-build post soaker, upend a section of drainpipe, plug the wider end with concrete, and fill it with preservative. The obvious limitation of this one is its small size.

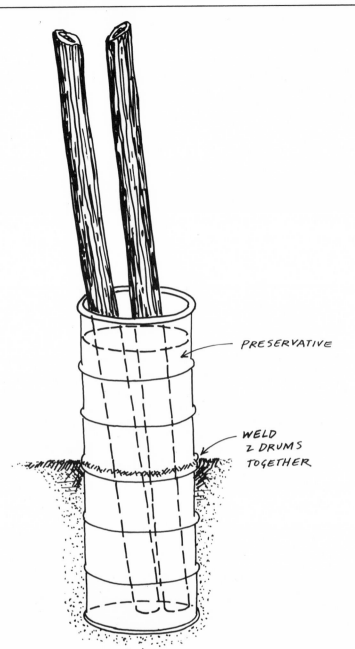

PRESERVATIVE

WELD
2 DRUMS
TOGETHER

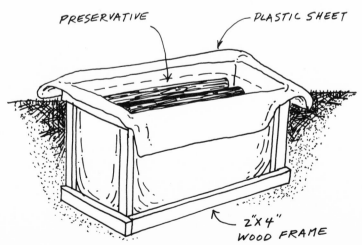

PRESERVATIVE

PLASTIC SHEET

2″X 4″
WOOD FRAME

# Gates

You'll want to plan before deciding on the gate you want for your fence. It should fit in with the style of your fence, and your garden.

But, no matter what style you choose, it should be:

- Wide enough for you and any equipment to get into the garden. Three feet wide is a minimum. Measure the widest cart or tiller you will be taking into the garden, and allow a minimum of six inches leeway.
- Sturdy. A child will swing on it and test it. You will bump into it with your garden cart. Adults will lean on it.
- Braced, so that it will not sag. The diagonal brace is usually a must.
- Hung on sturdy poles. Anchor them well. Think in terms of a 6"x6" post set three feet into the ground and held by concrete.
- Equipped with rustproof hardware.
- Built in some way so that the space between it and the ground does not permit entrance of the very animals you are trying to exclude.
- Built to open downhill, if your garden is on a slope. Otherwise it will bump into the uphill surface of your garden path.

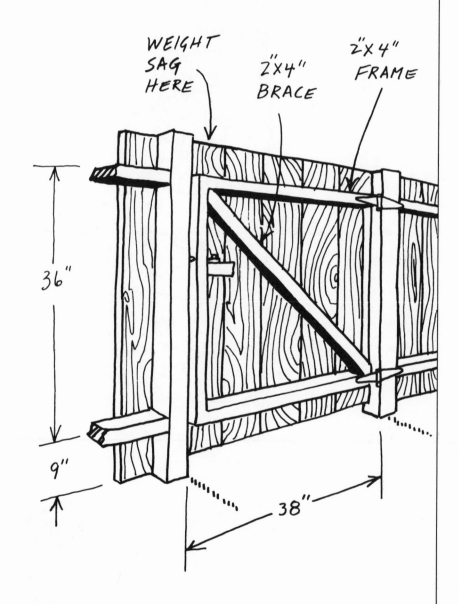

WEIGHT SAG HERE

2"X4" BRACE

2"X4" FRAME

36"

9"

38"

Here are two simple gates that illustrate some of those points. Note the framework is built of 2″x4″s to give it strength. Note the diagonal brace, running properly from the top of the swinging side of the gate to the bottom of the hinge-side. The posts are sturdy and held in place with concrete. Without those diagonals, this gate would have a tendency to sag at the top, making it difficult to open and shut. A gate with some such imperfection becomes a constant source of irritation.

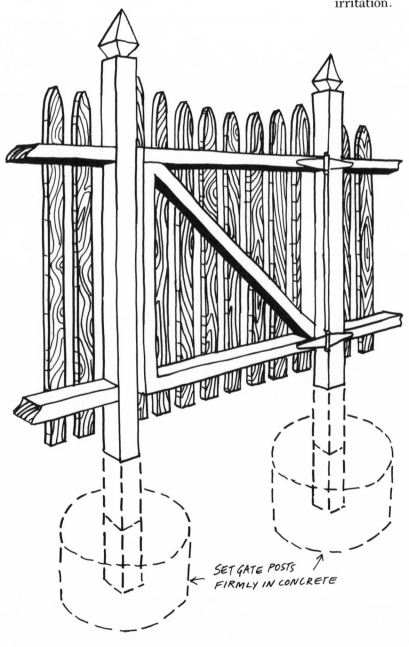

SET GATE POSTS FIRMLY IN CONCRETE

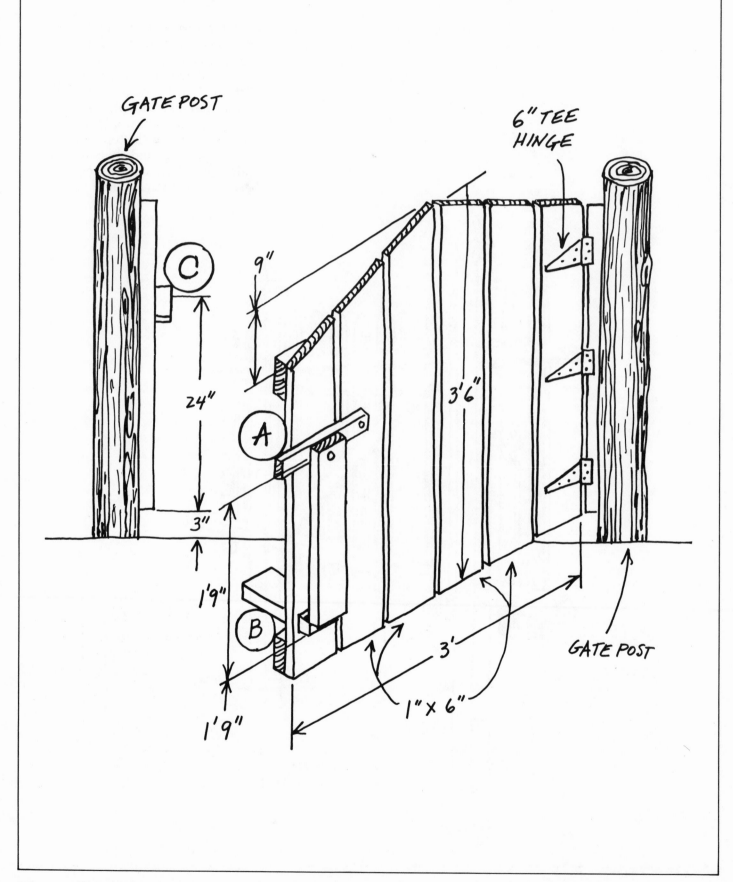

GATE POST

6" TEE HINGE

9"

C

24"

3'6"

A

3"

B

1'9"

3'

1"X6"

GATE POST

1'9"

# Foot-Operated Gate

If you often approach a gate with arms loaded, this is the gate for you. It is foot-operated, according to the Weyerhaeuser people who designed it. Note it is foot-operated on only one side and hand-operated on the other. Consider this when you install the gate. And, while these drawings do not show it, a diagonal brace is needed to prevent this from sagging.

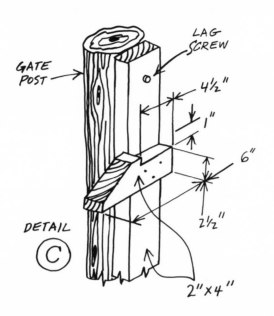

GATE POST

LAG SCREW

4½"

1"

6"

2½"

2"×4"

DETAIL Ⓒ

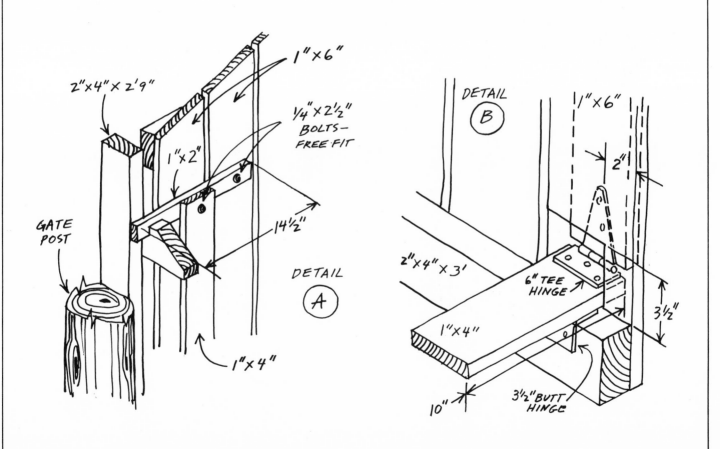

2"×4"×2'9"

1"×6"

¼"×2½" BOLTS—FREE FIT

1"×2"

GATE POST

14½"

DETAIL Ⓐ

1"×4"

DETAIL Ⓑ

1"×6"

2"

2"×4"×3'

6" TEE HINGE

3½"

1"×4"

10"

3½" BUTT HINGE

# Stone Fence Gate

If your ambition was so high that you created a stone wall, you have a slight problem in attaching a gate to it. Here's a relatively simple method, which involves anchoring 2"x6"s on both ends of the stone wall (make certain that lumber is installed at a true 90° with the ground). This can be done, as shown, by running lengthy screw eye bolts through the planks and cementing them into the wall. Gate is then hung as if those anchored planks were the fence posts.

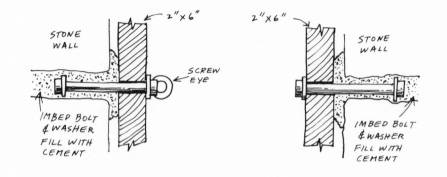

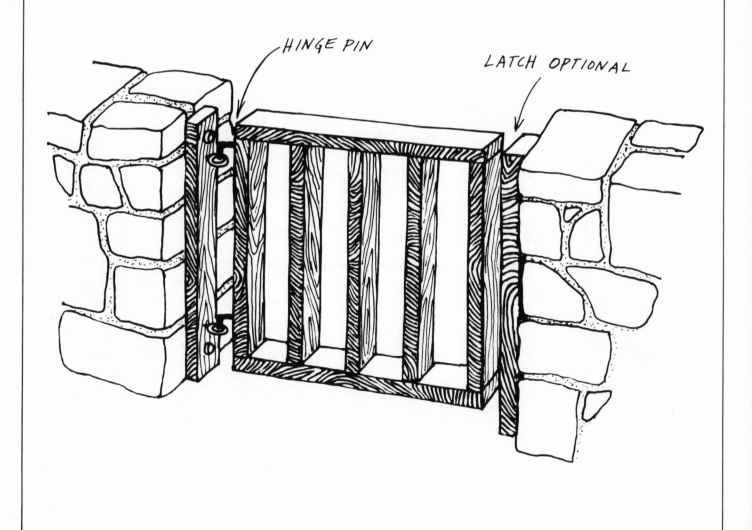

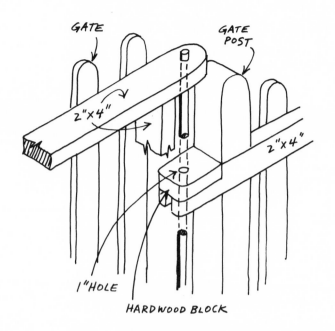

GATE

GATE POST

2"×4"

2"×4"

1"HOLE

HARDWOOD BLOCK

# Gate Hinge

This is where the true test of your gate takes place, right at the hinge. Is it strong enough to bear the weight of the gate? Does it bind in some disconcerting fashion? Does it squeak (something you might like or hate)?

Here's a simple way to hang a comparatively light gate.

Another easy method is to purchase three strap hinges, and make certain they are well mounted, for in all probability the gate will exert some pull against the screws holding the hinges in place.

If you can find and buy it, this hardware is excellent for the garden gate. The pin section is placed in the gatepost, and the ring section (use two of each for each gate) is placed in the gate itself, then the gate is put in place.

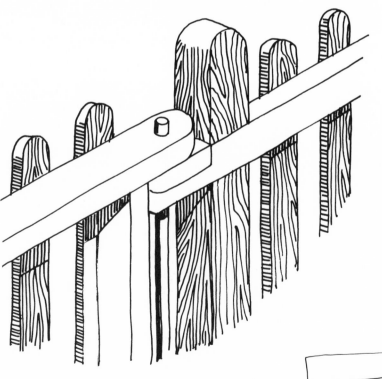

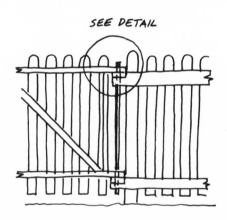

SEE DETAIL

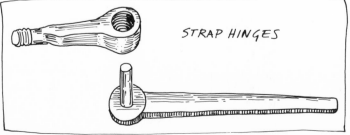

STRAP HINGES

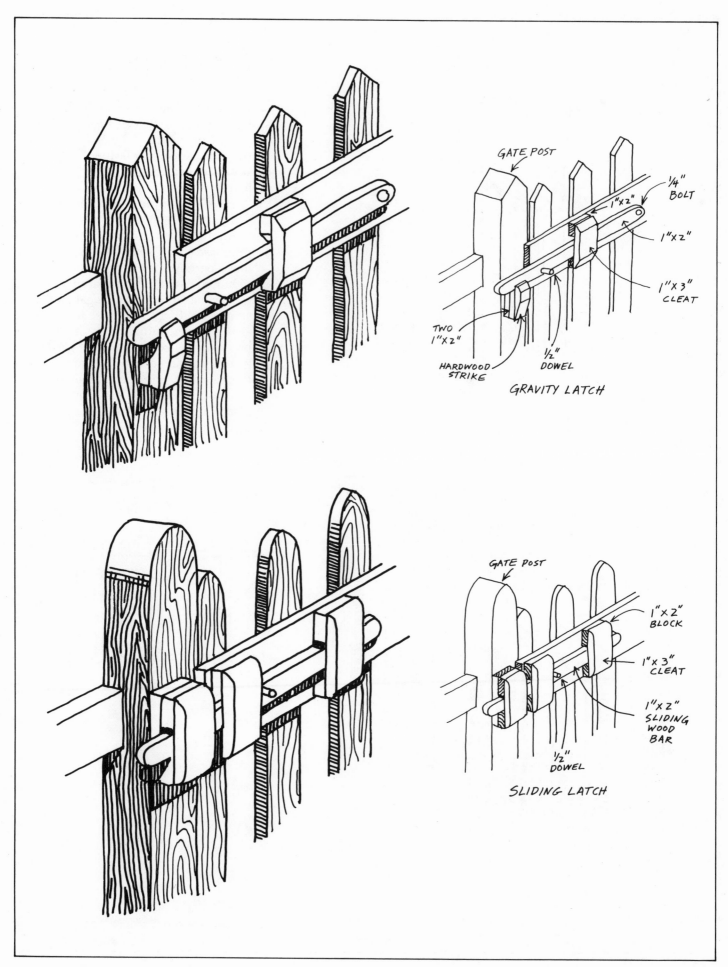

GATE POST

¼"
BOLT

1"×2"

1"×2"

1"×3"
CLEAT

TWO
1"×2"

HARDWOOD
STRIKE

½"
DOWEL

GRAVITY LATCH

GATE POST

1"×2"
BLOCK

1"×3"
CLEAT

1"×2"
SLIDING
WOOD
BAR

½"
DOWEL

SLIDING LATCH

# Gate Latches

You can purchase gate latches at your hardware store. But it's easy to build a latch that will be far more decorative. Here are a few simple ones, suggested by Weyerhaeuser Co., that can be made of wood.

SEE DETAIL

DROP LATCH GATE

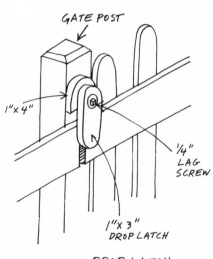

GATE POST

1" x 4"

1/4" LAG SCREW

1" x 3" DROP LATCH

DROP LATCH

# Stiles

A stile is a wonderful invention to save the wear and tear you will put on a fence if you crawl over, under or through it with any regularity. Use a stile only where the crossings are occasional. One to cross a fence between garden and compost pile would become a tiring nuisance. But one across a fence on a favorite walk through meadows can be a delight, and a place to rest and meditate a moment. Children love them. They can be houses, castles, or ships. A little-used one on a garden fence is ideal for potted plants—but only a few plants or you will trip the passers-up-and-over.

The person walking over a stile that puts him at fence-top height may find the altitude disconcerting. If so, mount a sturdy post beside the stile, and reaching up to at least four feet above it. Security—and an assist in balancing—is provided by it.

Here is a variety of models—all of them comparatively easy to build.

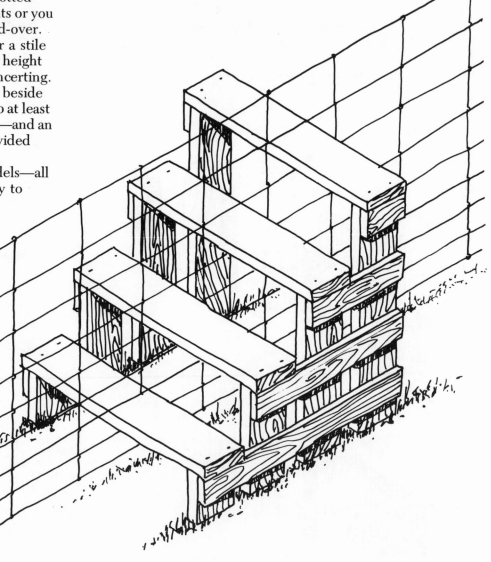

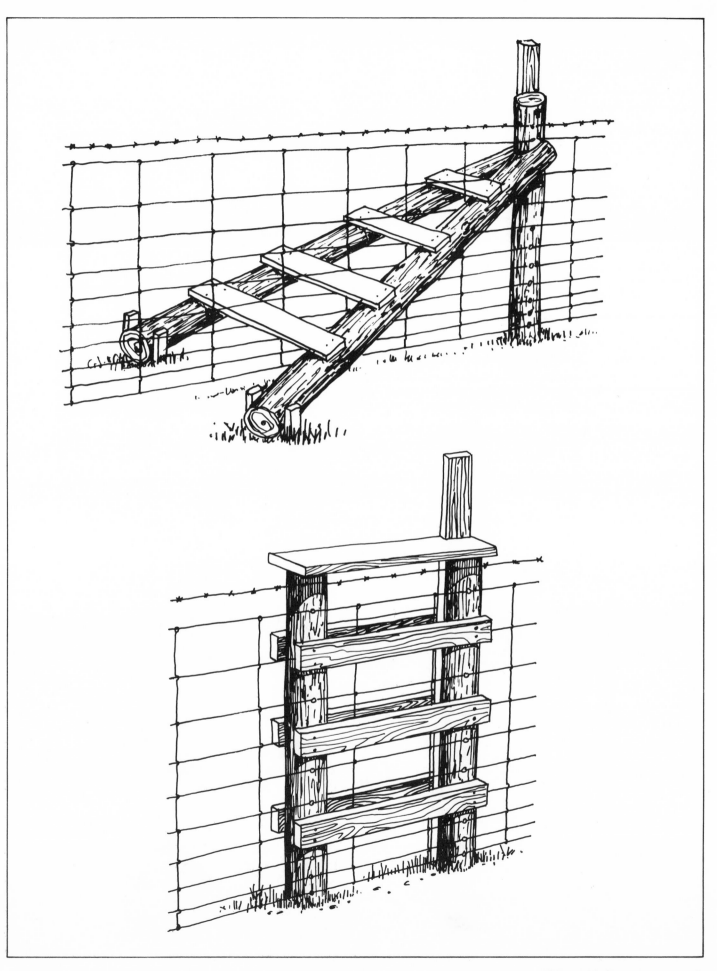

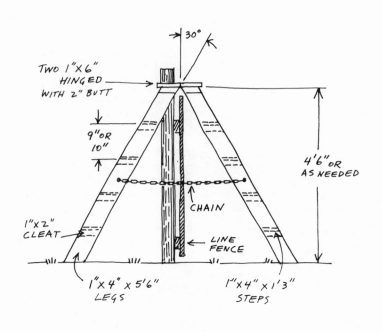

30°

TWO 1"X6"
HINGED
WITH 2" BUTT

9" OR
10"

4'6" OR
AS NEEDED

CHAIN

1"X2"
CLEAT

LINE
FENCE

1"X4" X 5'6"
LEGS

1"X4" X 1'3"
STEPS

1'6"

# Turnstile

TWO
2"X4" OR 2"X6"
ENDS & EDGES SANDED

DOUBLE DADO
GLUE TOGETHER
& SCREW FOR
BEST RESULTS

BOLT WITH
WASHERS

*IF* your garden entrance is purely decorative, and requires no gate to keep out dogs, cats, children beasts that prowl or yowl in the night . . . and *IF* you never enter your garden with wheelbarrows, tillers or other large and wheeled devices . . . and *IF* you are of modest horizontal dimensions . . . Then build a turnstile for your garden entrance.

Select a sturdy pole, soak it in wood preservative, and bury it at least three feet in the ground, for it will be pushed against and its strength will be tested by all children from ages 3 to 15. Likewise, make the crosspieces of sturdy stock, such as 2"x6", with edges and ends sanded smooth and round, and fasten it with a strong bolt. Several large washers placed between the cross and the post will insure easy turning.

A stile is charming and decorative, but, other than discouraging cows and horses and perhaps bears from entering your garden, it serves little useful purpose.

# Garden Bench

Every garden needs a bench. Put your trowel on it, and you won't waste time looking for it minutes later. Put your harvest on it, buckets of peas, fat squash, bunches of carrots. Put yourself on it, after hours of work, and contemplate the wonder of gardening, so much from such tiny seeds.

Here's a plan for a bench suggested by the California Redwood Association. It has many virtues. It can be built in less than an hour, but will last a lifetime. Its simple lines are pleasing.

It's made from an eight-foot 2″x12″ (or wider) and is braced with a 2″x4″. Cut two 14-inch pieces from the plank for legs, leaving a seat area 68 inches long. Center the 2″x4″ brace between the legs, glue with exterior-type glue and attach with ¼″x4″ countersunk flat-head wood screws. Attach legs to top by gluing and using same size screws. Finish to your own taste.

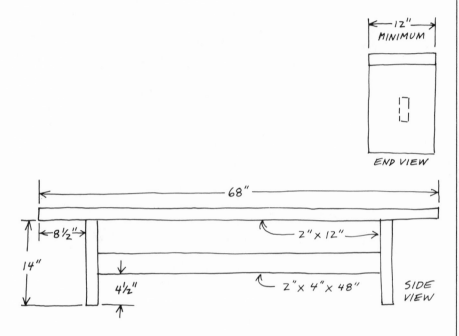

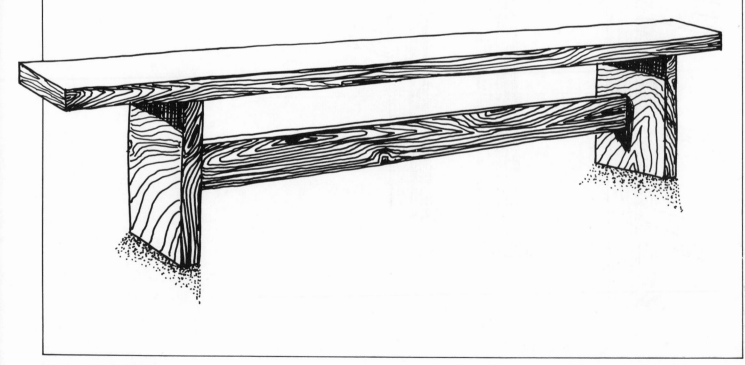

# Light Bench

Here's a much lighter bench that will fit well into a smaller garden. Its size and attractive lines make it adaptable to use inside the home as well as outside.

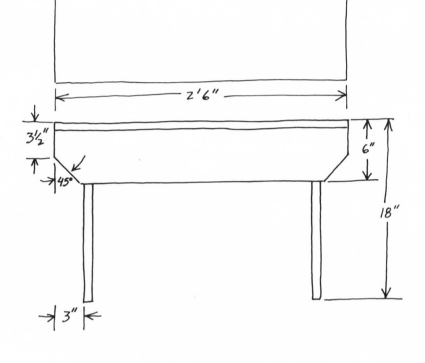

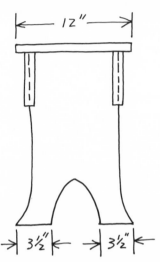

# Folding Bench

If your need is for a light bench, one that can be moved to various places, one that is easy to store for the winter, here it is, courtesy of Weyerhaeuser.

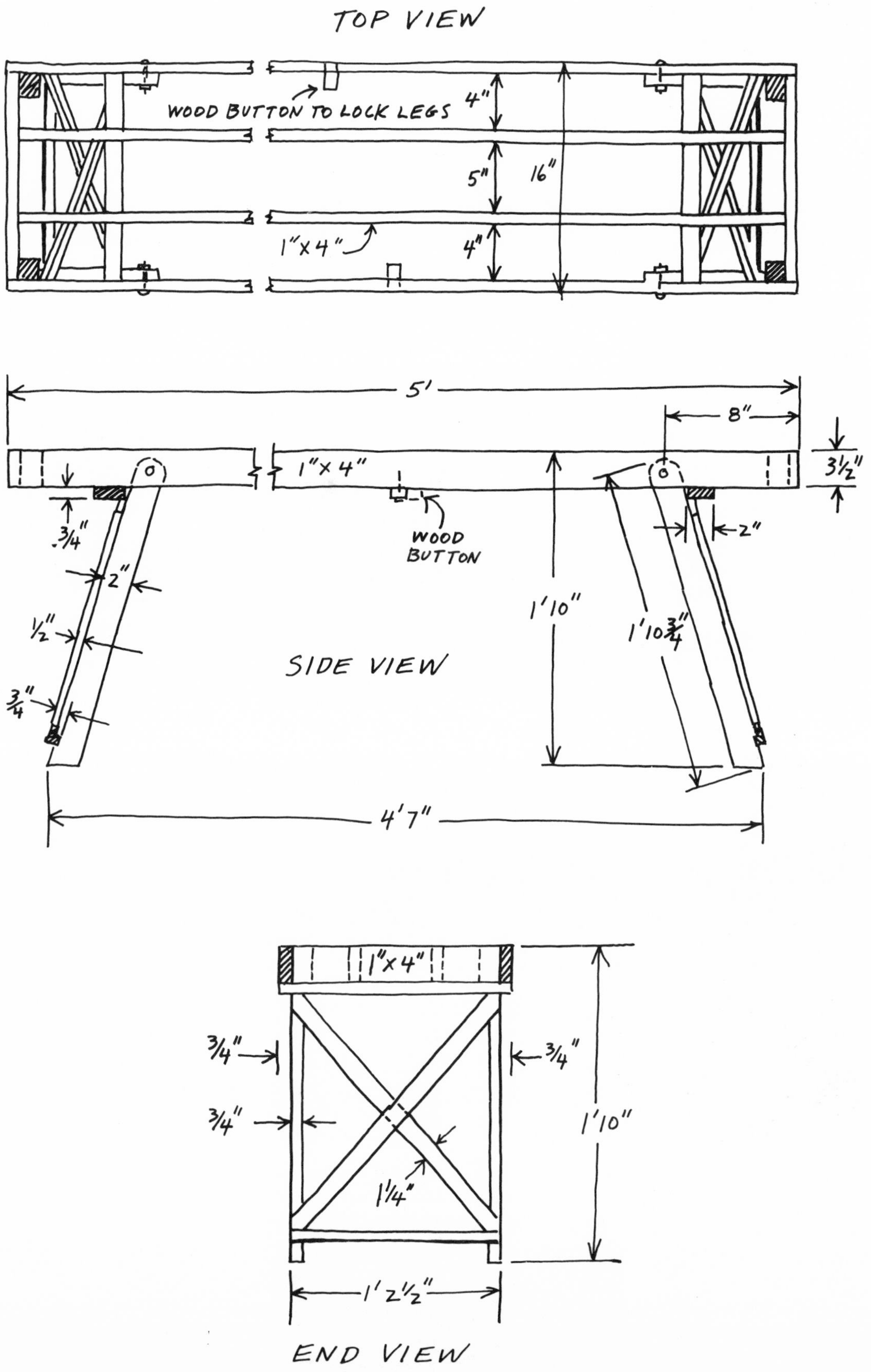

TOP VIEW

WOOD BUTTON TO LOCK LEGS   4"

5"   16"

1"x 4"   4"

5'

8"

3½"

1"x 4"

WOOD
BUTTON

3/4"

2"

½"

1'10"

1'10¾"

2"

3/4"

4'7"

SIDE VIEW

1"x 4"

3/4"   3/4"

3/4"   1'10"

1¼"

1'2½"

END VIEW

# Growing Grapes

For a satisfying venture, try growing grapes. There are varieties for nearly every section of the country. Grapes demand a minimum of care, and most of that is at a time that doesn't interfere with other gardening. They are remarkably free of disease.

Best of all is the harvest of grapes, eaten fresh, used in jellies or jams, or squeezed for the juice and the wine that may follow.

Look into a handbook on grapes and you will probably see the Kniffin system explained. This system has two wires between poles, one wire above the other, two hold the vine, pruned to four arms. The home gardener need not be tied down to such a system for his two or three vines. The first year of planting, the vine will need only a post, so the vine will be encouraged to grow upwards.

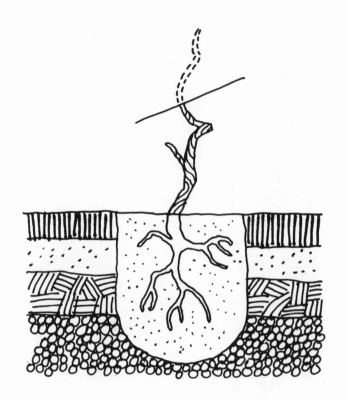

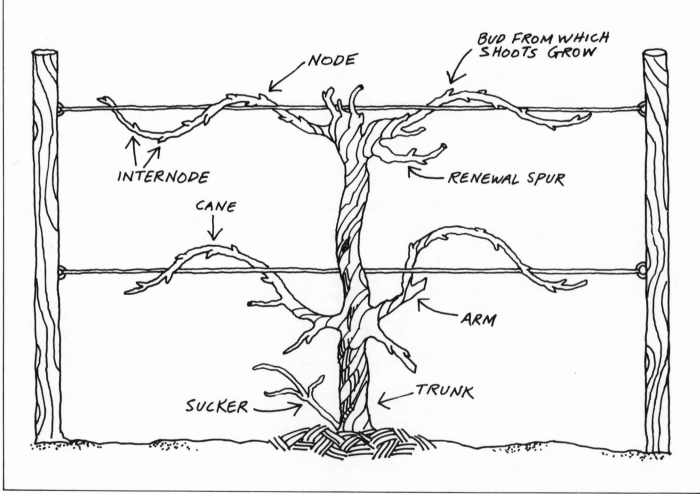

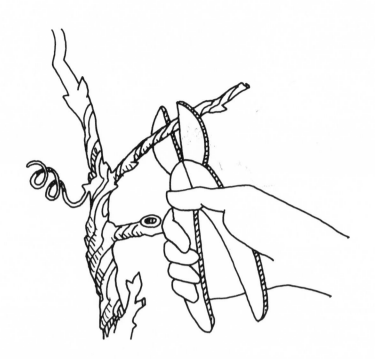

The second year a trellis will be needed. A simple way is to plant the vines eight feet apart, with stout poles set two and one-half feet into the ground, midway between the plants and, on the ends, four feet beyond the end plants. If the posts are eight feet long, one strand of wire (9 gauge galvanized is good) can stretch across the tops of the posts, and the second wire can be tied two feet below the top.

The weight of the vines puts an inward pull on those poles, particularly the end ones. They can be anchored with dead men or braced with a post, reaching from the top of each end post diagonally to the ground near the vine.

Grapes want sunshine, good air circulation (put rows eight feet apart) and rich soil. Provide these and you and your grandchildren will enjoy your vines.

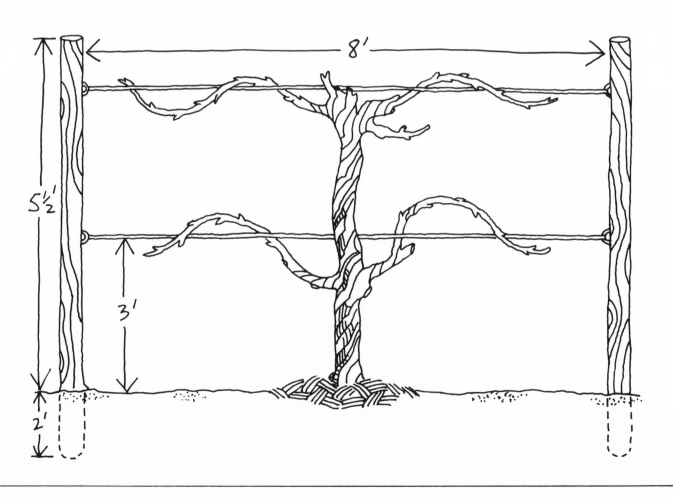

# Grapevine Building

Here's a delightful way to grow grapes, if your home or garage is built so there is a south-facing wall that can be used.

Supports are built out from the building, and connected with wire to support the grapevines.

This should be:

1. Sturdy. It will have a lot of weight on it when the vines stretch across and are heavy with grapes.
2. Built near enough to the ground so that the grapes can be picked.
3. If built under the slope of a roof, space should be left between the vines and the roof for runoff of rain and in cooler climates, the sliding of melting snow.

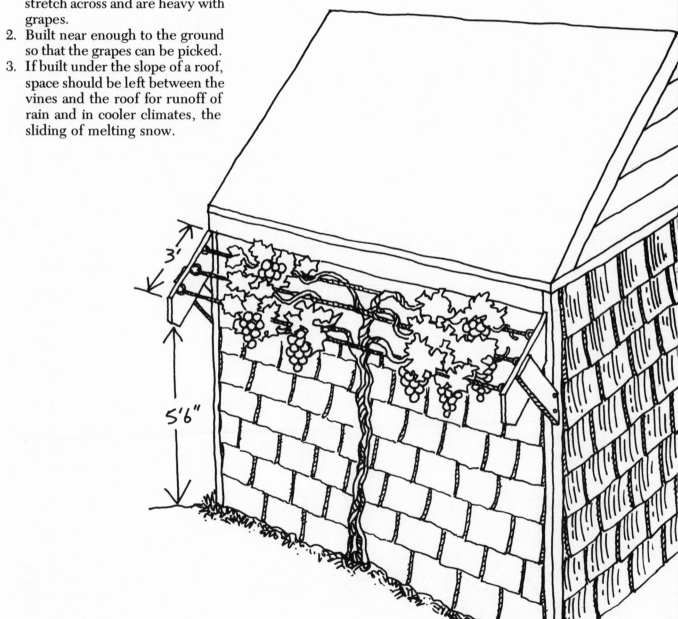

# Birdhouse

Before building a birdhouse, make a decision: Do you want more birds around your house and garden? They will give you a hand with the insect problems in the garden, but they also may help themselves to some of your produce, such as strawberries, grapes and cherries. There's no question but what birds are worth more than the food you may share with them, and their cheery presence definitely tips the scale in their favor.

If you want birds around your home and garden, birdhouses alone aren't enough. Plant some trees, shrubs or vines that offer them food, and they'll come a'flying.

If you're going to build, here are some suggestions:

1. Build for the bird's pleasure, not for your own. Don't paint the birdhouse with brilliant colors, and paint it at least a few weeks before the birds will occupy it, so the smell of paint will be gone.

2. Pick a site carefully. It should be safe from cats, the house should face away from the prevailing wind, and the house should not tilt upward, so that rain enters it. Don't place several houses for the same birds closely together. Birds have a strong territorial instinct, and several houses close together will only promote ill feelings among neighbors.

3. Build the house so its interior can be easily cleaned. This means hinging one side or the bottom so that it will swing open. Clean the house as soon as the birds desert it, and another couple may occupy it that summer.

4. Drill small holes in the bottom for drainage.

5. Use the proper dimensions and bore the correct size holes (see table) for entrance. Too large an entrance makes small birds vulnerable to attack or displacement by larger birds.

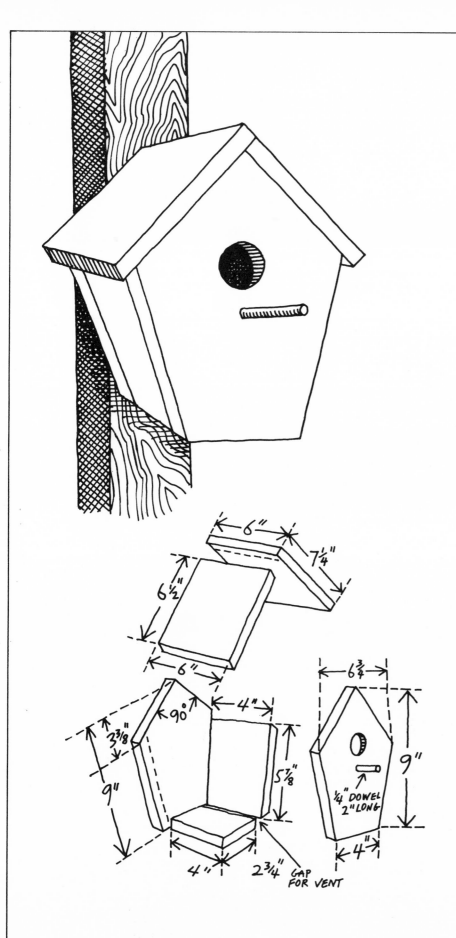

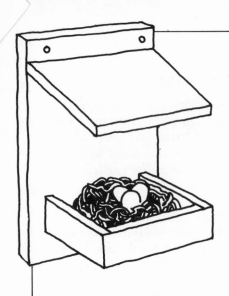

## A TABLE OF DIMENSIONS
### Nesting Shelves For Birds (One or more sides open)

| Kind of Bird | Min. Floor Size | Depth of Box | Preferred Height Above Ground |
|---|---|---|---|
| Robin | 6″ x 8″ | 8″ | 6′-15′ |
| Barn Swallow | 6″x6″ | 6″ | 8′-12′ |
| Song Sparrow | 6″x6″ | 6″ | 1′-3′ |
| Phoebe | 6″x6″ | 6″ | 8′-12′ |

### Birdhouse Dimensions

| Kind of Bird | Floor Size | Box Depth | Ht. of Entrance Above Floor | Diameter of Entrance | Height Above Ground |
|---|---|---|---|---|---|
| Bluebird | 5″x 5″ | 8″ | 6″ | 1½″ | 5′-10′ |
| Chickadee | 4″x 4″ | 8″-10″ | 6″- 8″ | 1⅛″ | 6′-15′ |
| Titmouse | 4″x 4″ | 8″-10″ | 6″- 8″ | 1¼″ | 6′-15′ |
| Nuthatch | 4″x 4″ | 8″-10″ | 6″- 8″ | 1¼″ | 12′-20′ |
| Wrens: House and Bewick's | 4″x 4″ | 6″- 8″ | 4″- 6″ | 1″-1¼″ | 6′-10′ |
| Carolina | 4″x 4″ | 6″- 8″ | 4″- 6″ | 1¼″ | 6′-10′ |
| Violet Greenswallow and Tree Swallow | 5″x 5″ | 6″ | 1″- 5″ | 1½″ | 10′-15′ |
| Purple Martin | 6″x 6″ | 6″ | 1″ | 2½″ | 15′-20′ |
| House Finch | 6″x 6″ | 6″ | 4″ | 2″ | 8′-12′ |
| Starling | 6″x 6″ | 16″-18″ | 14″-16″ | 2″ | 10′-25′ |
| Crested Flycatcher | 6″x 6″ | 8″-10″ | 6″- 8″ | 2″ | 8′-20′ |
| Flicker | 7″x 7″ | 16″-18″ | 14″-16″ | 2½″ | 6′-20′ |
| Woodpeckers: Golden Fronted, Redheaded | 6″x 6″ | 12″-15″ | 9″-12″ | 2″ | 12′-20′ |
| Downy | 4″x 4″ | 8″-10″ | 6″- 8″ | 1¼″ | 6′-20′ |
| Hairy | 6″x 6″ | 12″-15″ | 9″-12″ | 1½″ | 12′-20′ |
| Owls: Screech | 8″x 8″ | 12″-15″ | 9″-12″ | 3″ | 10′-30′ |
| Saw-whet | 6″x 6″ | 10″-12″ | 8″-10″ | 2½″ | 12′-20′ |
| Barn | 10″x18″ | 15″-18″ | 4″ | 6″ | 12′-18′ |
| Sparrow hawk | 8″x 8″ | 12″-15″ | 9″-12″ | 3″ | 10′-30′ |
| Wood duck | 10″x18″ | 10″-24″ | 12″-16″ | 4″ | 10′-20′ |

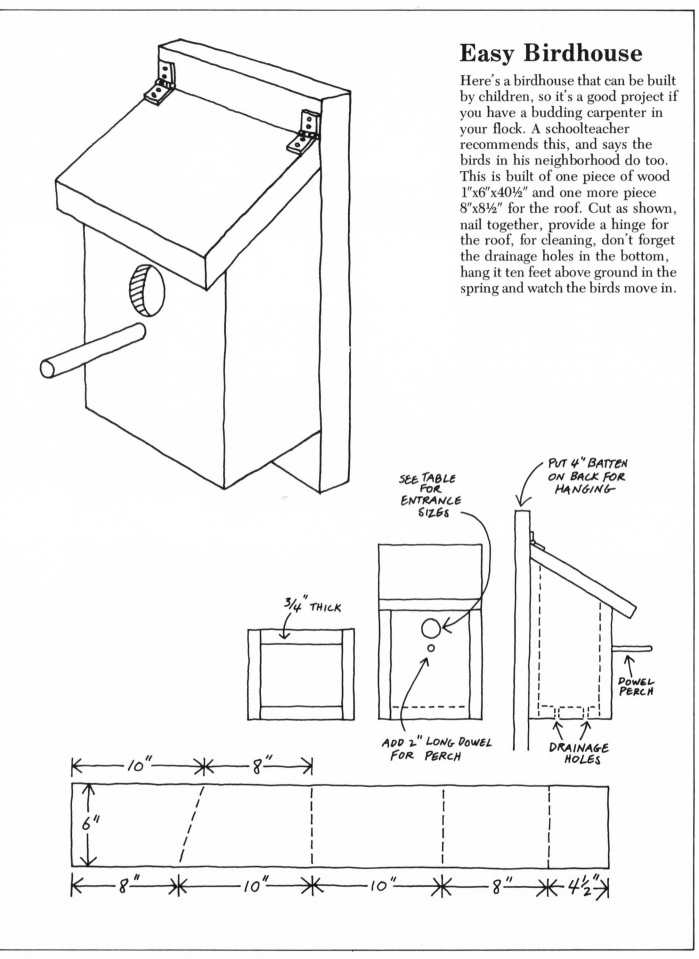

# Easy Birdhouse

Here's a birdhouse that can be built by children, so it's a good project if you have a budding carpenter in your flock. A schoolteacher recommends this, and says the birds in his neighborhood do too. This is built of one piece of wood 1"x6"x40½" and one more piece 8"x8½" for the roof. Cut as shown, nail together, provide a hinge for the roof, for cleaning, don't forget the drainage holes in the bottom, hang it ten feet above ground in the spring and watch the birds move in.

SEE TABLE FOR ENTRANCE SIZES

PUT 4" BATTEN ON BACK FOR HANGING

3/4" THICK

ADD 2" LONG DOWEL FOR PERCH

DOWEL PERCH

DRAINAGE HOLES

10"    8"

6"

8"    10"    10"    8"    4½"

# Robin's Shelf

Robins do not like the confinement of a birdhouse. And they are particularly careless about their choice of a nest location. They will build where there is much human traffic, then complain loudly about that traffic keeping their young nervous and awake. Help them solve their problems with a shelf that provides a roof over their heads, sides for partial protection and an 8″ square base for the nest.

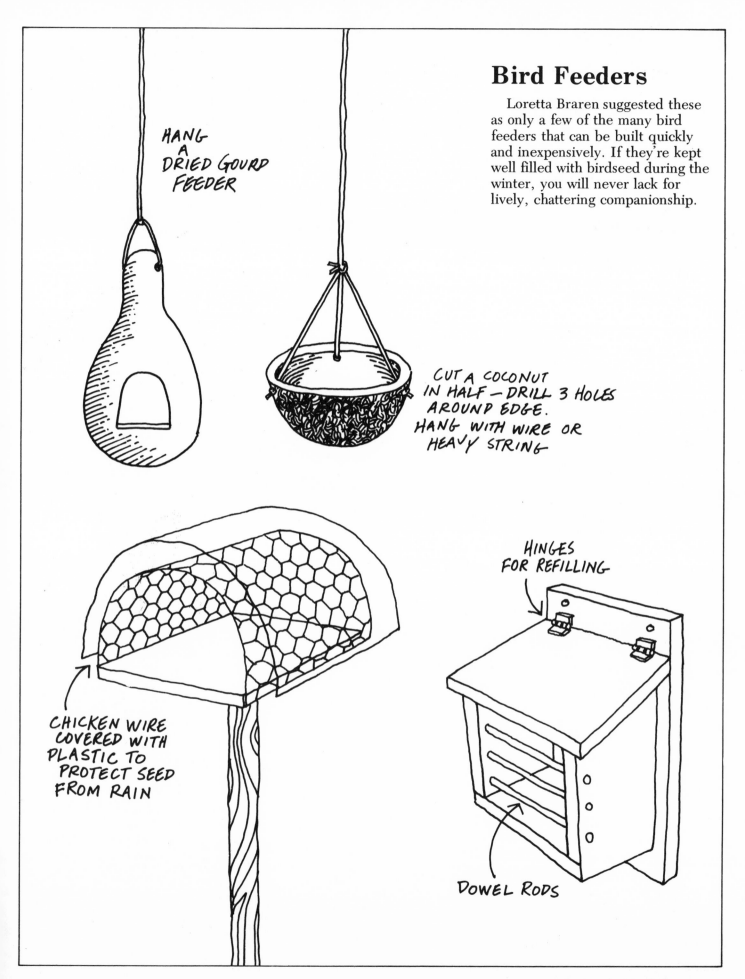

## Bird Feeders

Loretta Braren suggested these as only a few of the many bird feeders that can be built quickly and inexpensively. If they're kept well filled with birdseed during the winter, you will never lack for lively, chattering companionship.

HANG A DRIED GOURD FEEDER

CUT A COCONUT IN HALF — DRILL 3 HOLES AROUND EDGE. HANG WITH WIRE OR HEAVY STRING

HINGES FOR REFILLING

CHICKEN WIRE COVERED WITH PLASTIC TO PROTECT SEED FROM RAIN

DOWEL RODS

# Part 3

# EASY~
# TO~MAKE
# THINGS
# FOR YOUR
# FARM

# Hog House

This hog house is a one-litter unit designed for on-pasture use to provide shelter in both summer and winter. The American Plywood Association developed it to be built from three and one-half sheets of ⅜-inch exterior plywood with a 2'x6' base and 2'x3' framing. Put it on a high part of the pasture, for better ventilation, and have it face into the south and the sunlight in the winter and the opposite direction in the summer. It features a door in the roof, which again will help with ventilation during the warm days. And move it at least 300 feet away from your home—or anyone else's.

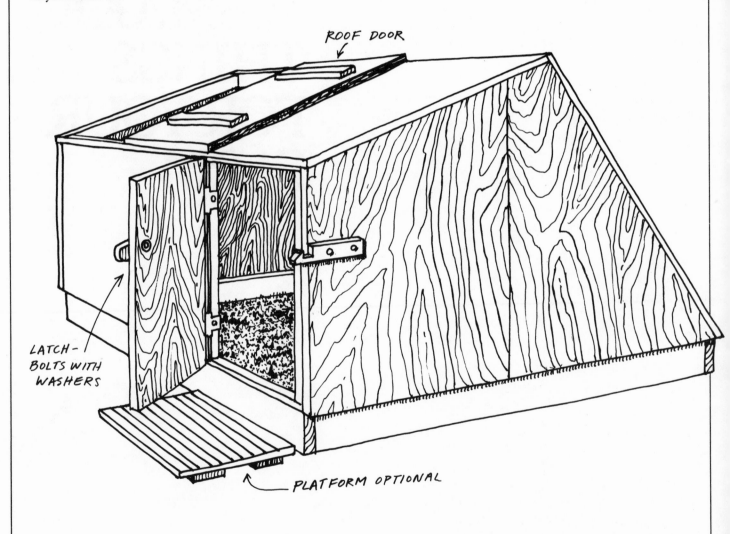

ROOF DOOR

LATCH-
BOLTS WITH
WASHERS

PLATFORM OPTIONAL

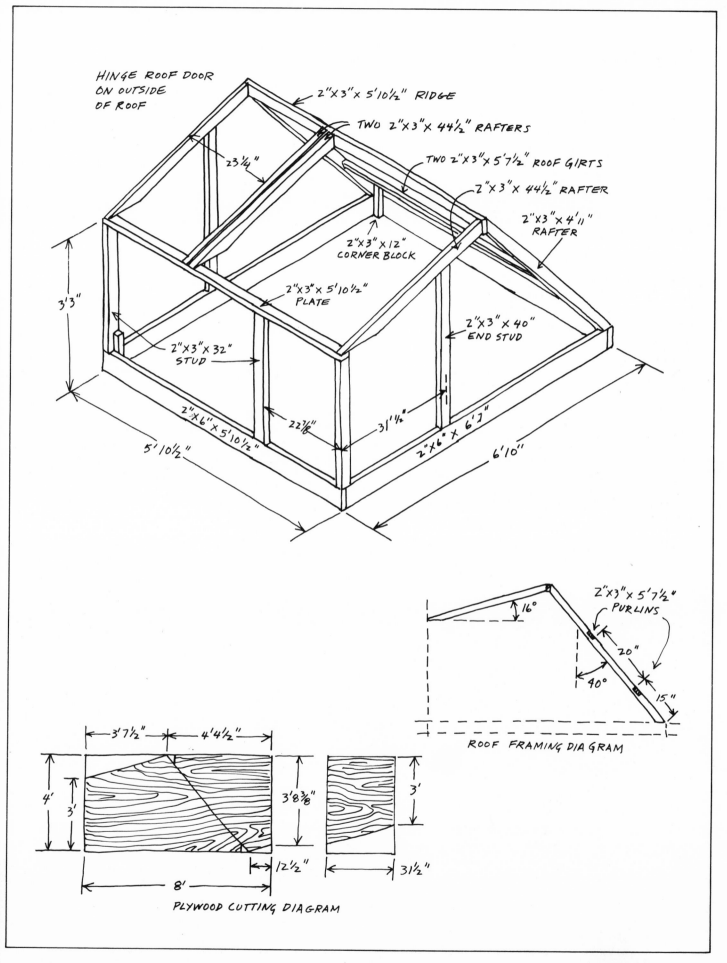

HINGE ROOF DOOR
ON OUTSIDE
OF ROOF

2"x3"x 5'10½" RIDGE

TWO 2"x3"x 44½" RAFTERS

TWO 2"x3"x 5'7½" ROOF GIRTS

2"x3"x 44½" RAFTER

2"x3"x 4'11" RAFTER

23¼"

2"x3"x 12" CORNER BLOCK

3'3"

2"x3"x 5'10½" PLATE

2"x3"x 40" END STUD

2"x3"x 32" STUD

2"x6"x 5'10½"

22⅞"

31'½"

2"x6" x 6'2"

5'10½"

6'10"

ROOF FRAMING DIAGRAM

2"x3"x 5'7½" PURLINS

16°

20"

40°

15"

PLYWOOD CUTTING DIAGRAM

3'7½"

4'4½"

4'

3'

3'8⅜"

3'

12½"

31½"

8'

# Pig Feeder

The things that can happen when you're feeding pigs. Some of them won't happen if you construct this feeder. Make certain you don't provide an escape route for your pigs with this. Install posts for the spout unit. Be sure the spout is well braced. If you cut wires to install this, secure the loose ends tightly to the spout unit.

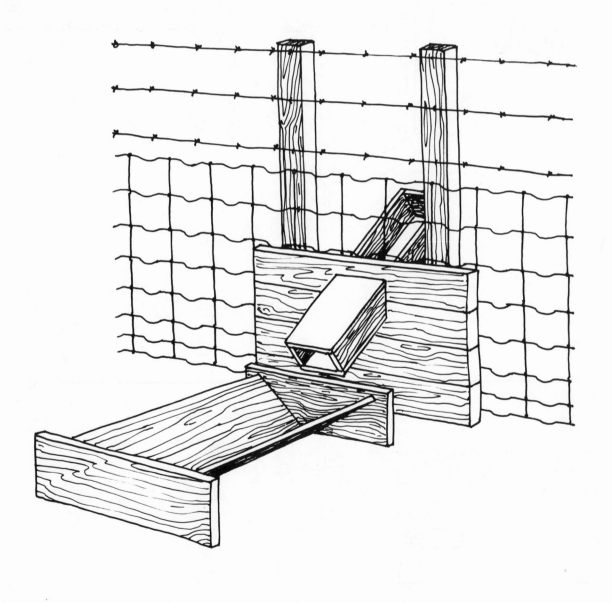

## Movable Shed

Here's a shed that could answer many of your needs. Want a storage shed, or a place for handling large amounts of garden produce, or a roadside stand, or a workshop, or . . .?

This is the building you need. It's a roomy 12′x12′, has a broad side door and a front that will open up and out of the way. Three press-preservative treated timbers, 4″x4″x13′, are used as skids.

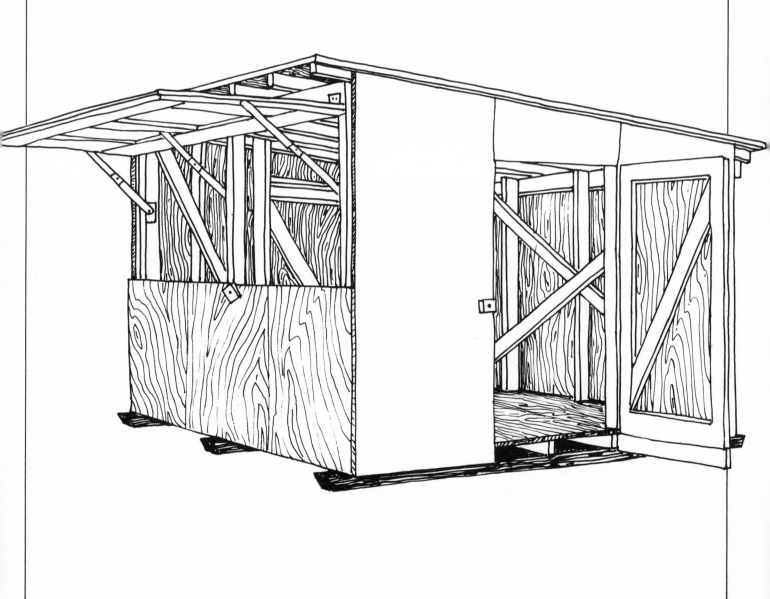

Wooden cross braces, 1″x6″ x 16′x 3″ are notched into the skids and floor joists, and then secured with ten penny common nails. The floor joists, placed two feet on center, are fastened to the skids with steel framing anchors, metal straps or ⅜″ diameter bolts. Corner posts are 2″x4″ double studs, staggered and spaced sixteen inches on center. They are fastened to the skids with steel framing anchors and metal straps.

The walls are built of 2″x4″ studs with 1″x4″ braces notched into them. This provides a strong, smooth surface for the exterior covering. Roof joists are spaced two feet apart. Exterior-type plywood or many other materials might be chosen for the floor, walls and roof.

This design is from West Virginia University, and has been published by the U.S. Department of Agriculture as its Plan 6099.

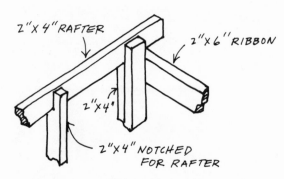

ROOF — CORNER POST DETAIL

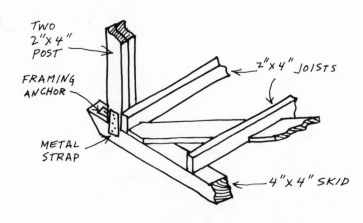

FLOOR — CORNER POST DETAIL

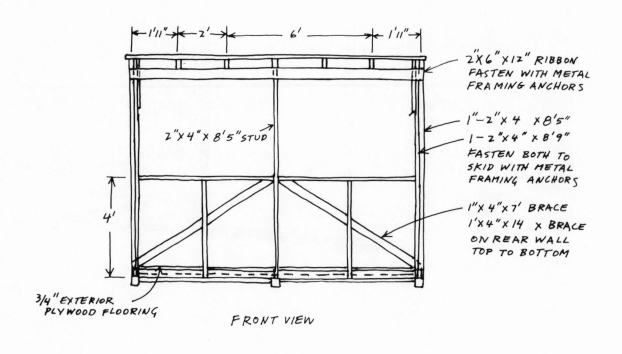

FRONT VIEW

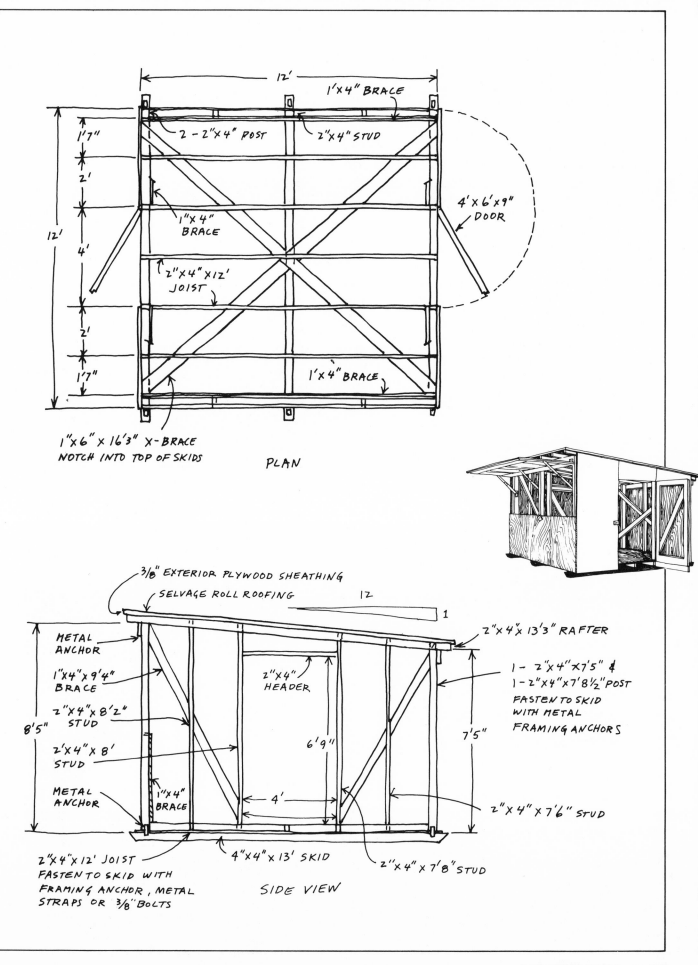

12'

1'×4" BRACE

1'7"

2 - 2"×4" POST

2"×4" STUD

2'

4'×6'×9'
DOOR

1"×4"
BRACE

12'

4'

2"×4"×12'
JOIST

2'

1'7"

1'×4" BRACE

1"×6" × 16'3" X-BRACE
NOTCH INTO TOP OF SKIDS

PLAN

3/8" EXTERIOR PLYWOOD SHEATHING

SELVAGE ROLL ROOFING

12

1

2"×4"×13'3" RAFTER

METAL
ANCHOR

1"×4"×9'4"
BRACE

2"×4"
HEADER

1 - 2"×4"×7'5" &
1 - 2"×4"×7'8½" POST
FASTEN TO SKID
WITH METAL
FRAMING ANCHORS

2"×4"×8'2"
STUD

8'5"

2'×4"× 8'
STUD

6'9"

7'5"

METAL
ANCHOR

1"×4"
BRACE

4'

2"×4"×7'6" STUD

2"×4"×12' JOIST
FASTEN TO SKID WITH
FRAMING ANCHOR , METAL
STRAPS OR 3/8" BOLTS

4"×4" × 13' SKID

2"×4" × 7'8" STUD

SIDE VIEW

# Hog Fence

Since the Troy-Bilt Roto Tiller is one of the products of the Garden Way family, it is difficult for us to think anything can do a job that will equal the work done by that tiller.

But for preparing meadowland or any other soddy area for gardening, the pig will give the tiller a good run for its money.

The Roto Tiller will do the job more quickly, it's true. And there won't be any irate neighbors complaining about its smell.

It has its drawbacks. The Roto Tiller won't root down into the ground and eat up every last weed root that's there. Its exhaust won't read .55 percent in nitrogen content and almost as high in phosphate and potash. And whoever tried butchering a Troy-Bilt in the fall?

To have a pig do this job for you requires a pen that can be moved, or a stout fence around the entire area where you want to garden next year.

For a pen that can be moved, make four sides, each four feet high and ten feet long, and with 1"x6" rough boarding bolted on as slats so the breezes can move through it but the pig can't. That's heavy, but you need the strength in each section. Wire these sections together to form the pen. That way, it can be taken apart and moved with a minimum of fuss.

You'll need a small pen, too, that you can set over the pig during those daily moves. Combine the move with a treat—grain—for the pig and there should be cooperation from all concerned.

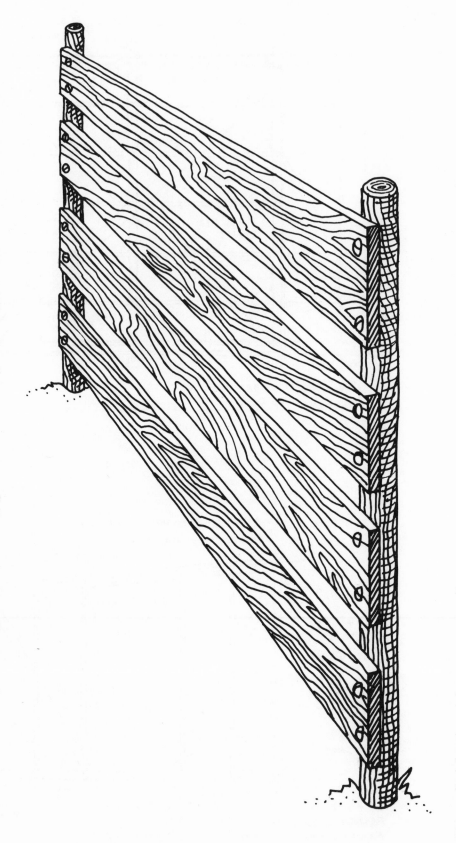

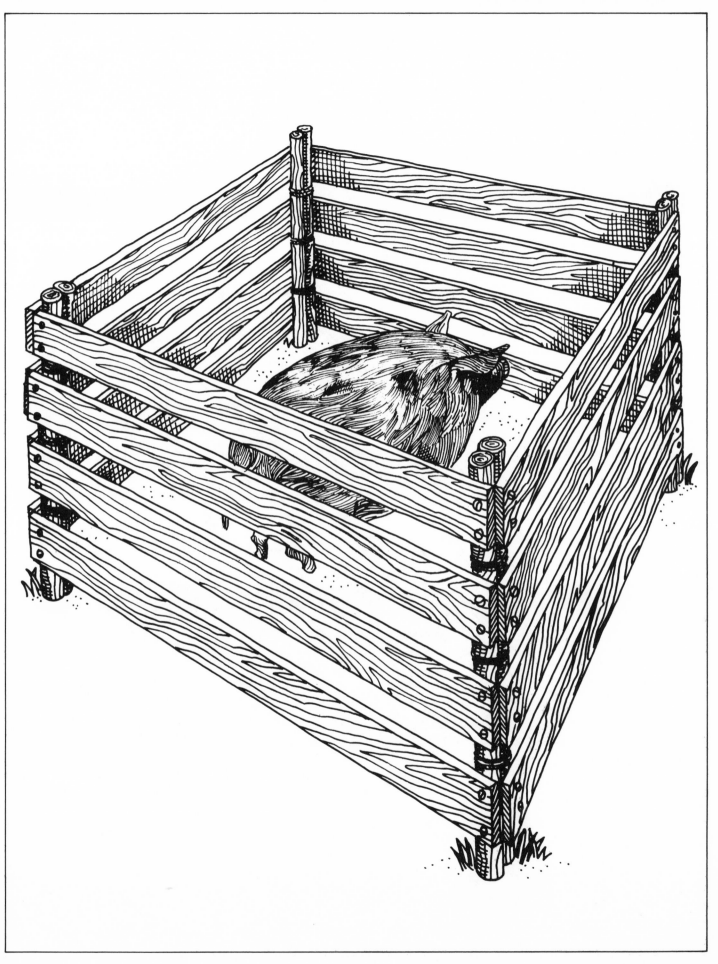

# Movable Loading Chute

This chute will quickly pay for itself
in time-saving, lack of injured
animals and all-round convenience.
Height of top of plank floor should
be level with bed of your truck.
Note floor reinforcements, 12″
distance between hardwood cleats
(at fourteen inches on center).

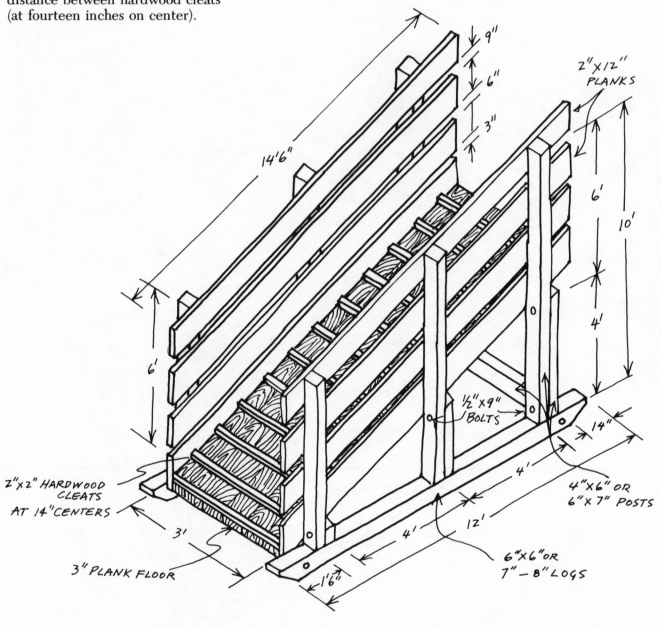

# Portable Horse Stable

This portable, one-horse stable was designed at Rutgers University and has been published by the U.S. Department of Agriculture as its Plan 6082 to meet the growing demand across the nation for housing for a single riding horse. Ventilation is provided by openings between the rafters at the front and rear, plus two hinged panels in the rear wall, and a Dutch door.

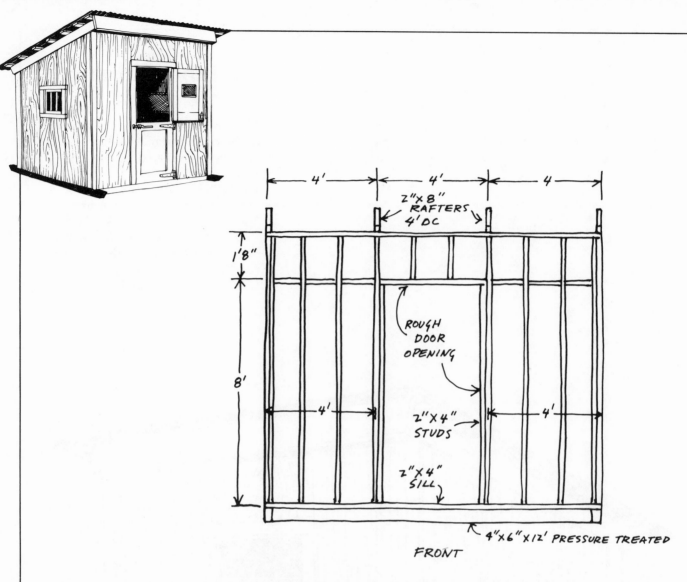

4'   4'   4

2"X8" RAFTERS 4'OC

1'8"

8'

ROUGH DOOR OPENING

4'   4'

2"X4" STUDS

4'   4'

2"X4" SILL

4"X6"X12' PRESSURE TREATED

FRONT

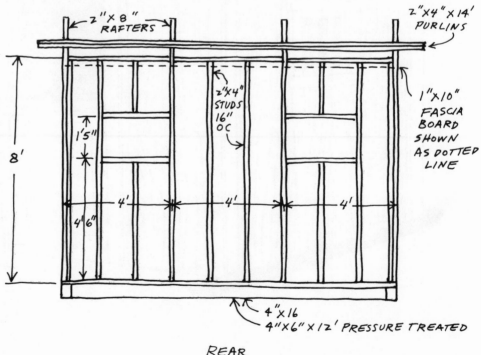

2"X8" RAFTERS

2"X4"X14' PURLINS

2"X4" STUDS 16" OC

1"X10" FASCIA BOARD SHOWN AS DOTTED LINE

8'

1'5"

4'   4'   4'

4'6"

4"X16
4"X6"X12' PRESSURE TREATED

REAR

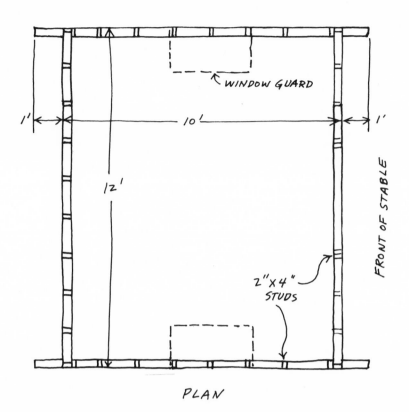

WINDOW GUARD

1'

10'

1'

12'

FRONT OF STABLE

2"X4" STUDS

PLAN

The stable has no floor covering, but well-tamped clay is suggested. It should be several inches higher than the outside ground level.

Construction is simple. The wall panels are framed and finished on the ground, then raised and secured to the timber base. The exterior-type plywood siding stiffens the walls and eliminates the need for let-in braces. The roofing is corrugated metal and translucent plastic.

Don't use paint containing lead on any part of this building.

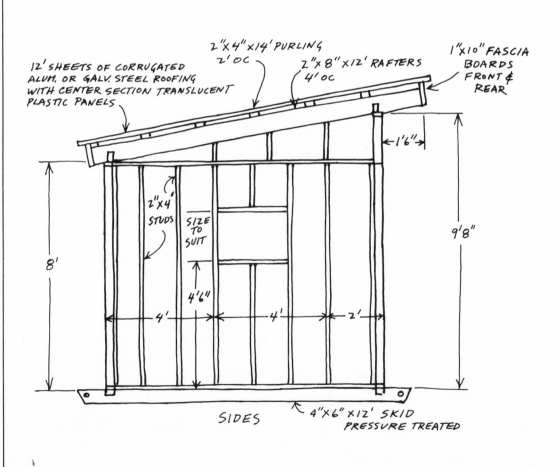

2"X4"X14' PURLING 2' OC

2"X8"X12' RAFTERS 4' OC

1"X10" FASCIA BOARDS FRONT & REAR

12' SHEETS OF CORRUGATED ALUM. OR GALV. STEEL ROOFING WITH CENTER SECTION TRANSLUCENT PLASTIC PANELS

1'6"

2"X4" STUDS

SIZE TO SUIT

9'8"

8'

4'6"

4'

4'

2'

SIDES

4"X6"X12' SKID PRESSURE TREATED

# Corral Gate

Here's a gate that's built to take it. Note it is made of heavy materials, yet is hung with a diagonal brace so weight is balanced and will not drag. A rake tooth is used as a spring to hold slider that locks gate in closed position. Not shown is latch post, with strap iron to hold end of slider. Use ⅜" machine bolts, not nails, in construction. Gate post must be heavy. Set it at least three feet in ground, with concrete holding it firm.

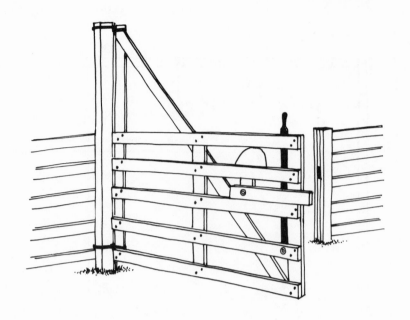

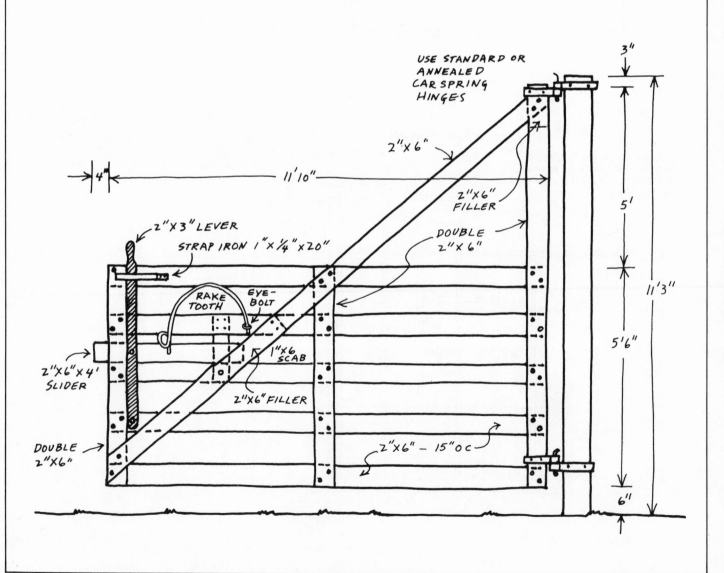

# Goat Milking Stand

Here's a milking stand for goats that considers your comfort as well as the comfort of the goat. Goats quickly adapt to it and you'll find it beats squatting to milk, particularly if you have several does to milk.

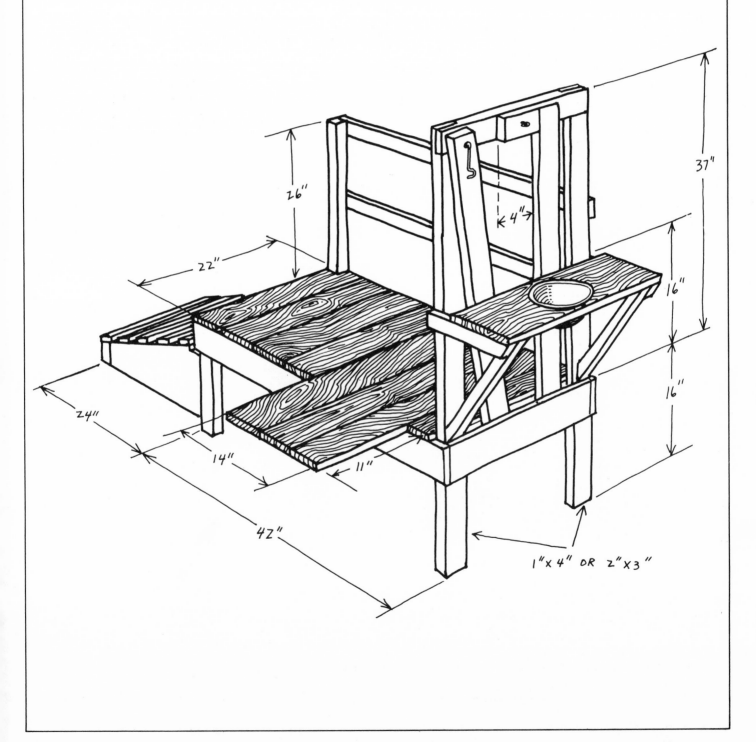

# Watering Trough

Here's a U.S. Department of Agriculture plan for a watering trough that can be recommended for cattle. It is sturdy, will last for years, little can go wrong with it, and, important on a hot day, it is roomy. Six cows can belly up to this bovine bar.

The basic part of this trough is a concrete pipe four feet in diameter. First, install the drain tile and water supply, then fit couplings flush with the top of the finished floor of the trough. Set the concrete pipe in place in a shallow circular trench dug around the drain as the center. Tamp pipe into place, and grade area to drain away from the trough. Pour concrete to form platform around the trough as well as the trough bottom. Leave a half-inch expansion joint between the concrete pipe and the platform.

The overflow and the supply pipes are screwed into the couplings cast into the floor of the trough. The two-inch overflow pipe is protected from clogging with a four-inch protective sleeve, held in place with ⅛"x1" steel brackets.

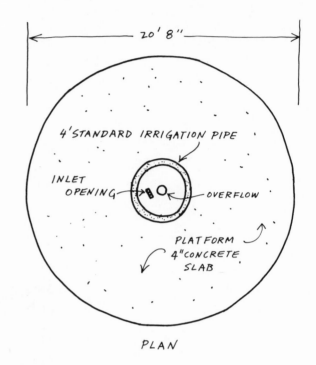

PLAN

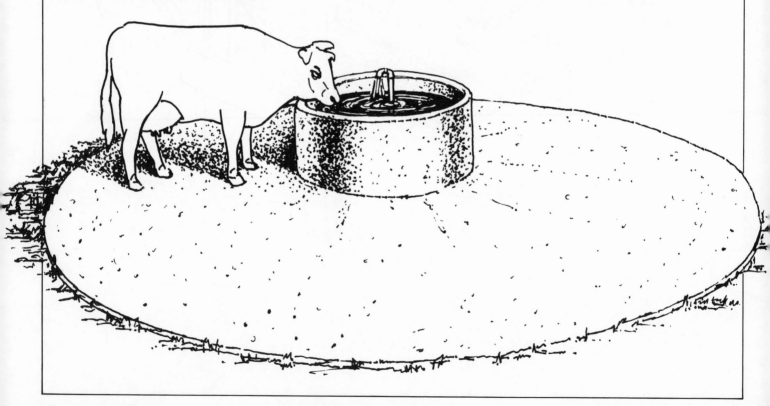

The lower brackets are welded to the overflow pipe and the upper brackets to the protective sleeve so the sleeve will slip off the overflow pipe. This permits removal of the overflow with a pipe wrench.

Should this trough be placed in the shade? USDA says no. That encourages the cattle to loaf near the water and does little to keep the water cool.

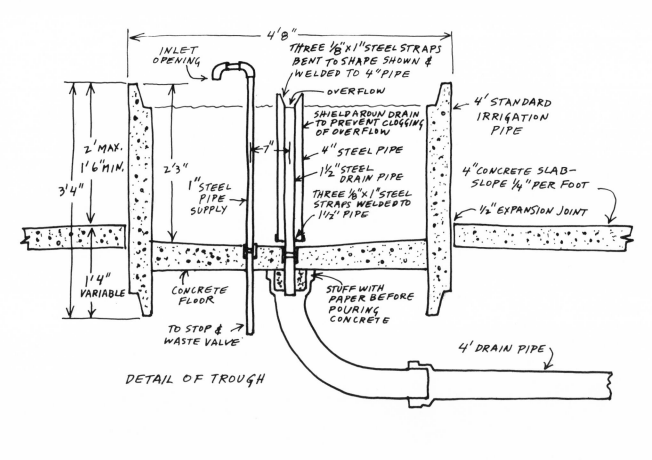

INLET OPENING

4' 8"

THREE ⅛"×1" STEEL STRAPS BENT TO SHAPE SHOWN & WELDED TO 4" PIPE

OVERFLOW

SHIELD AROUND DRAIN TO PREVENT CLOGGING OF OVERFLOW

4' STANDARD IRRIGATION PIPE

4" STEEL PIPE

1½" STEEL DRAIN PIPE

THREE ⅛"×1" STEEL STRAPS WELDED TO 1½" PIPE

4" CONCRETE SLAB—SLOPE ¼" PER FOOT

½" EXPANSION JOINT

2' MAX.
1' 6" MIN.

3' 4"

2' 3"

7"

1" STEEL PIPE SUPPLY

1' 4" VARIABLE

CONCRETE FLOOR

STUFF WITH PAPER BEFORE POURING CONCRETE

TO STOP & WASTE VALVE

4' DRAIN PIPE

DETAIL OF TROUGH

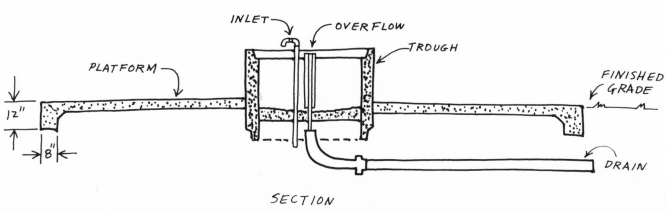

INLET

OVERFLOW

TROUGH

PLATFORM

FINISHED GRADE

12"

8"

DRAIN

SECTION

# Poultry House

This is an ideal house for a small flock, and for the person who prefers floor housing instead of the cage systems used today by most commercial egg producers. It will provide clean, dry housing throughout the year, can be ventilated, should be insulated in northern climates, and, handy for the poultryman, has a small storage room.

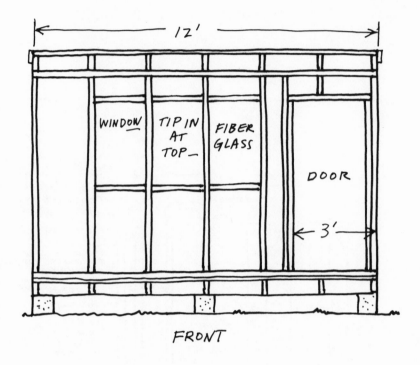

FRONT

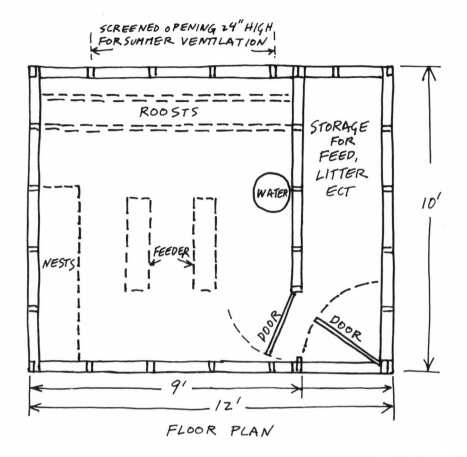

SCREENED OPENING 24" HIGH
FOR SUMMER VENTILATION

ROOSTS

STORAGE
FOR
FEED,
LITTER
ECT

WATER

NESTS

FEEDER

DOOR

DOOR

10'

9'

12'

FLOOR PLAN

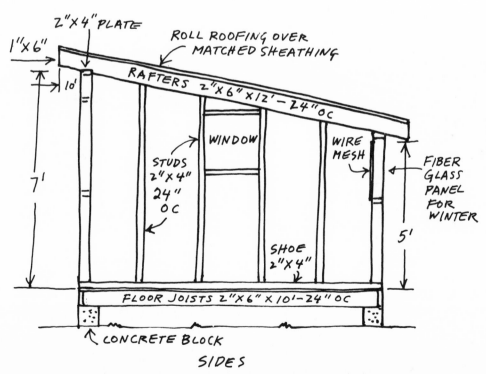

2"X4" PLATE

1"X6"

ROLL ROOFING OVER
MATCHED SHEATHING

RAFTERS 2"X6"X12' — 24" OC

10'

WINDOW

STUDS
2"X4"
24"
OC

WIRE
MESH

FIBER
GLASS
PANEL
FOR
WINTER

7'

SHOE
2"X4"

5'

FLOOR JOISTS 2"X6" X 10'—24" OC

CONCRETE BLOCK

SIDES

# Chicken Feeders

Leonard Mercia, writing in his *Raising Poultry the Modern Way*, stresses that feeders should be large enough to supply the flock's needs for a day or more without wasting feed. The design of the feeder is closely tied to the control of waste. Devices to prevent waste include an anti-roost spring on top of the feeder, and a lip on the side of the hopper to prevent birds from beaking out feed. If the feeder is never more than half-filled, much feed will be saved.

Here are three feeders you can build.

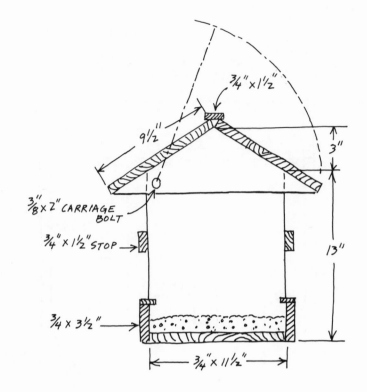

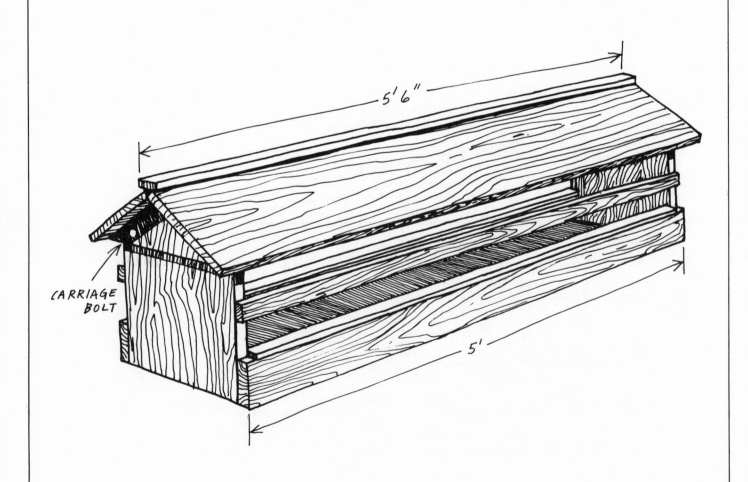

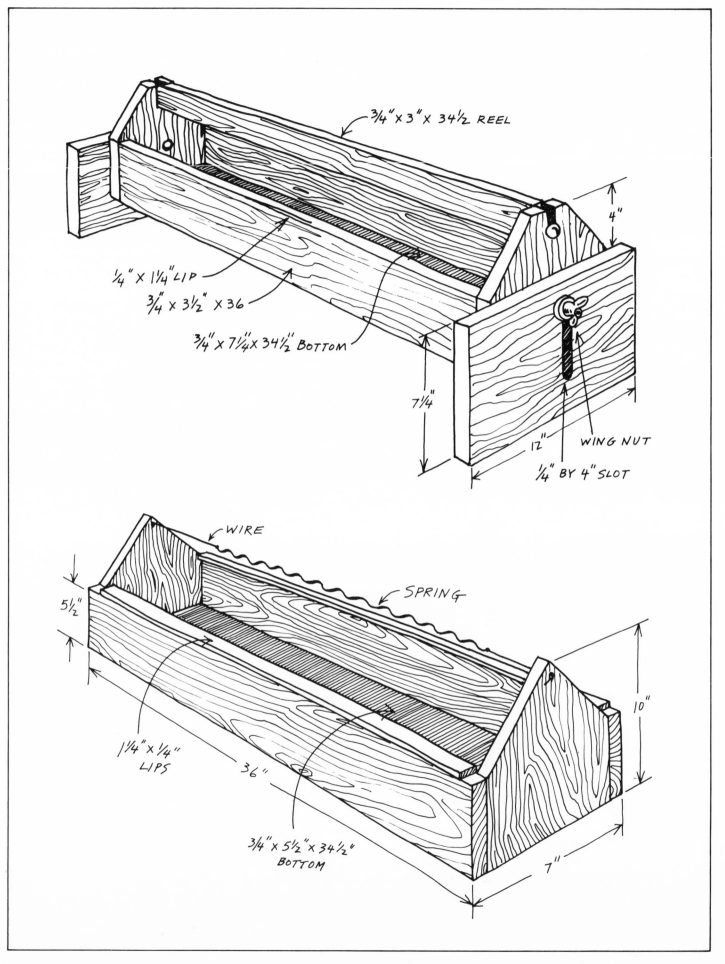

3/4" x 3" x 34 1/2 REEL

4"

1/4" x 1 1/4" LIP

3/4" x 3 1/2" x 36

3/4" x 7 1/4" x 34 1/2" BOTTOM

7 1/4"

12"

WING NUT

1/4" BY 4" SLOT

WIRE

SPRING

5 1/2"

10"

1 1/4" x 1/4" LIPS

36"

3/4" x 5 1/2" x 34 1/2" BOTTOM

7"

# Waterers

Hens and chickens must have access to clean, fresh water at all times. Laying birds will drink about a quart of water for every pound of feed consumed, and the amount of water will be much higher in hot weather.

The waterer made from a gallon can and a pan works very well for a small flock.

If you have running water piped into the house, you will probably buy an automatic water fountain, and eliminate one task from your list of daily chores. If you do, place it on this platform you can build of five pieces of 1"x4"x30", nailed into a square as shown and covered with 1"x2" mesh welded wire. It will provide dryer conditions around the fountain, and lessen the amount of litter material that finds its way into the fountain

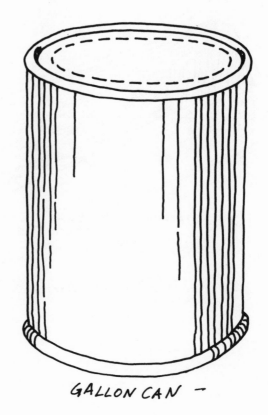

GALLON CAN —

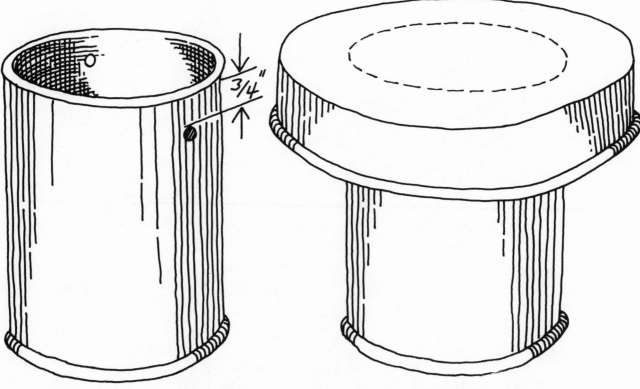

3/4"

ADD HOLES — AND WATER — PLACE PAN ON TOP —

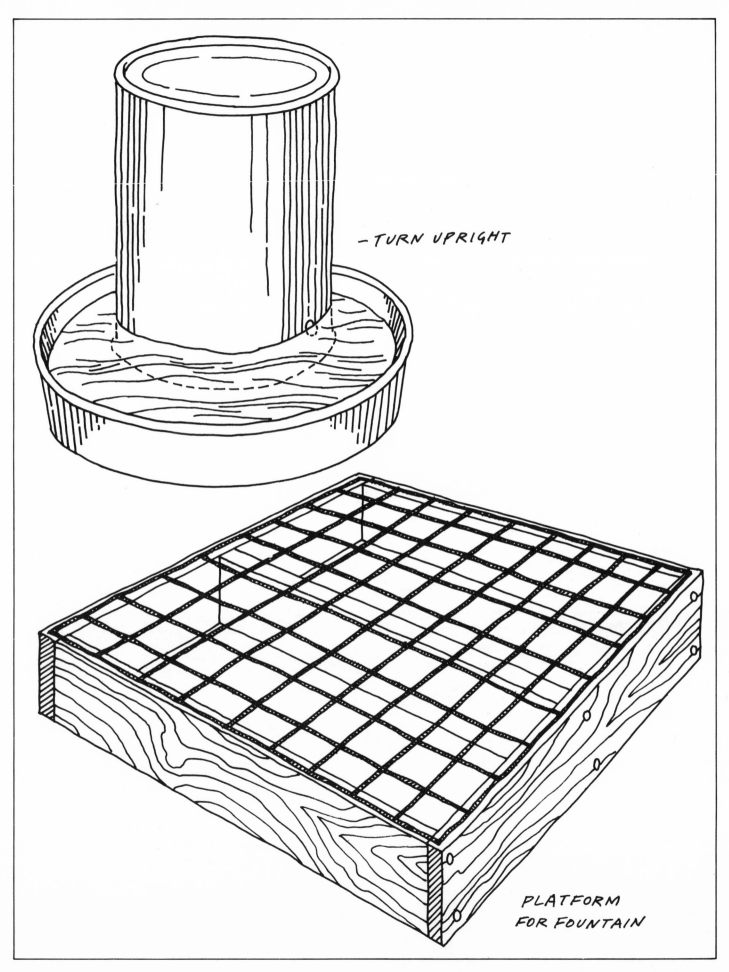

—TURN UPRIGHT

PLATFORM
FOR FOUNTAIN

# Brooder

If you're going to start day-old chickens, you'll need a brooder to keep them warm. Here is one you can build yourself. You can select one of the two alternate heating methods shown.

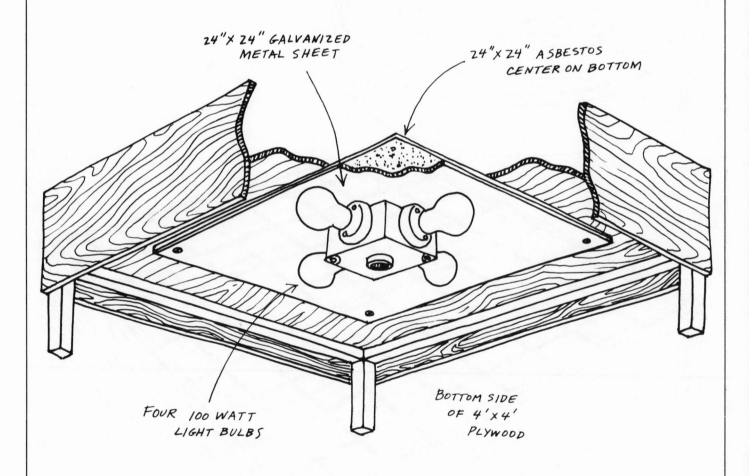

24" X 24" GALVANIZED METAL SHEET

24" X 24" ASBESTOS CENTER ON BOTTOM

FOUR 100 WATT LIGHT BULBS

BOTTOM SIDE OF 4' X 4' PLYWOOD

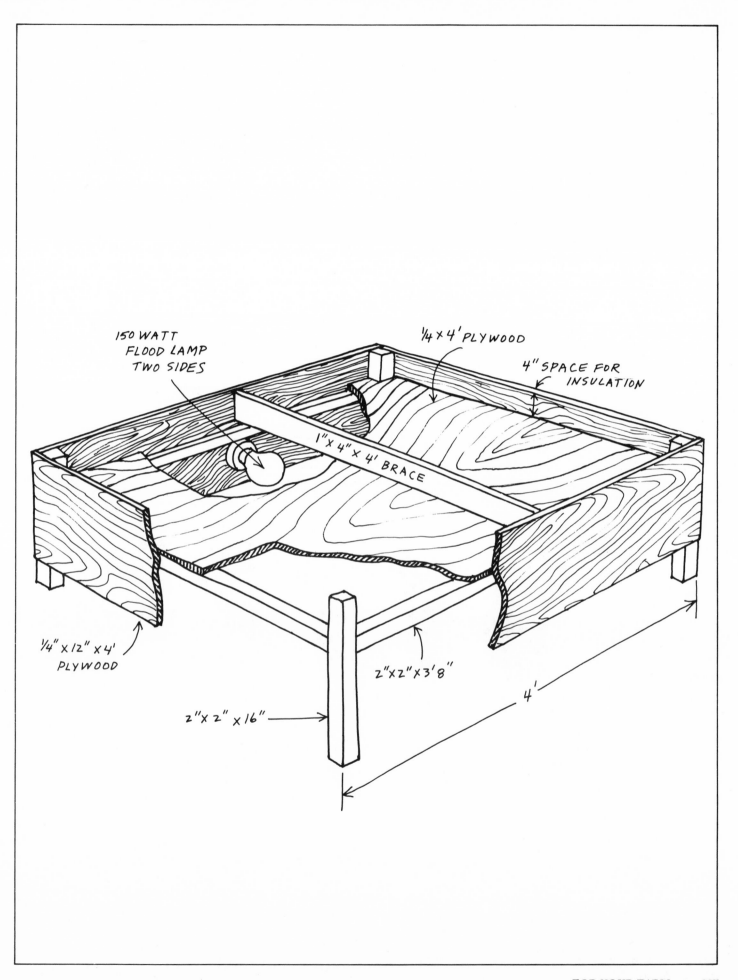

150 WATT
FLOOD LAMP
TWO SIDES

¼ X 4' PLYWOOD

4" SPACE FOR
INSULATION

1" X 4" X 4' BRACE

¼" X 12" X 4'
PLYWOOD

2" X 2" X 3' 8"

2" X 2" X 16"

4'

# Nests

You'll need one individual nest, or one square foot of community nest, for every four laying birds in your flock. Leonard Mercia recommends that individual nests be at least one foot in length, width and height. For community nests, provide two 9"x12" openings for each twenty square feet of nest space. Provide a landing board in front of all openings, and have nests about two feet above the floor.

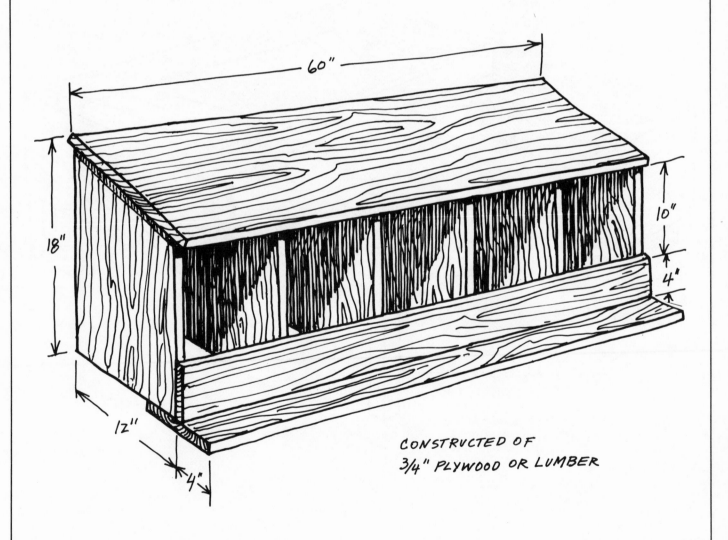

CONSTRUCTED OF
3/4" PLYWOOD OR LUMBER

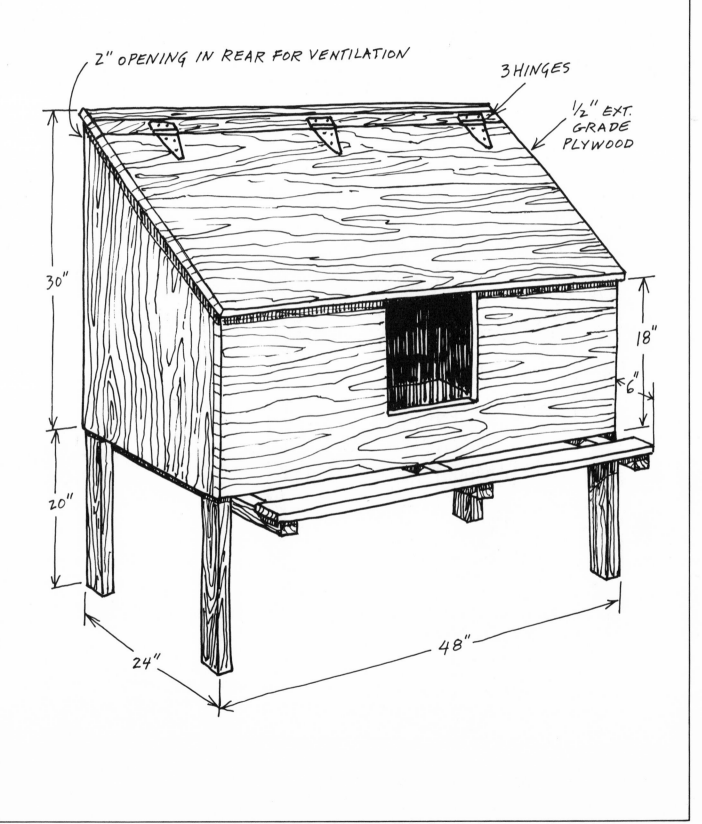

2" OPENING IN REAR FOR VENTILATION

3 HINGES

½" EXT. GRADE PLYWOOD

30"

18"

6"

20"

24"

48"

# Egg Candling Light

Eggs are candled to determine whether they are fertile. The infertile egg will appear clear before the light. If much candling is to be done, a candling light such as this will speed the task.

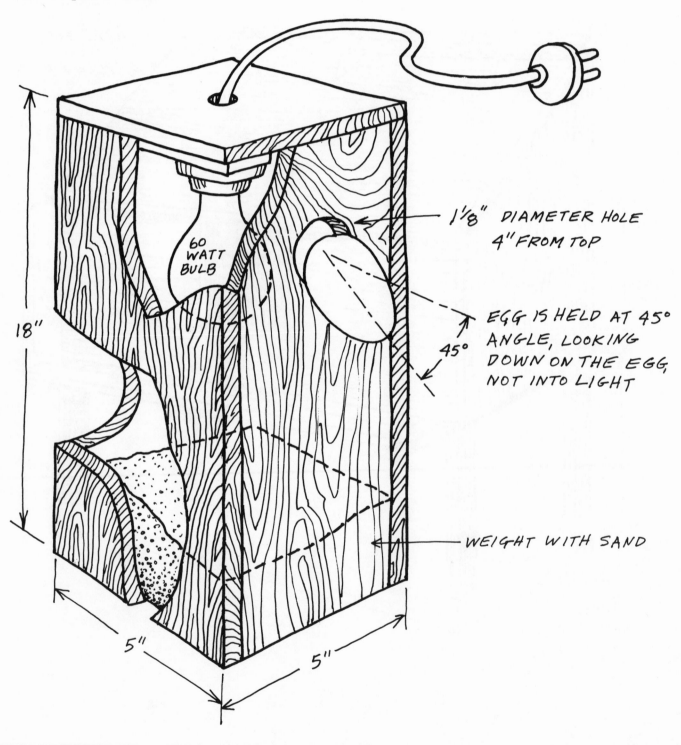

60 WATT BULB

18"

5"

5"

1 1/8" DIAMETER HOLE 4" FROM TOP

EGG IS HELD AT 45° ANGLE, LOOKING DOWN ON THE EGG, NOT INTO LIGHT

45°

WEIGHT WITH SAND

# Incubator

A good setting hen provides ideal incubating conditions for nine or ten eggs. To duplicate these conditions requires some careful work, since temperature, ventilation and humidity are important.

The temperature must be between 100° and 103° F. and should be held at 102°. Humidity during the initial period of the 21 days of incubation varies from 83° to 88° F. (wet bulb thermometer) depending on the type of eggs. The level is increased to 90-95° F. (wet bulb) in the last three or four days before hatching.

If such exact work is within your capabilities, try building this incubator.

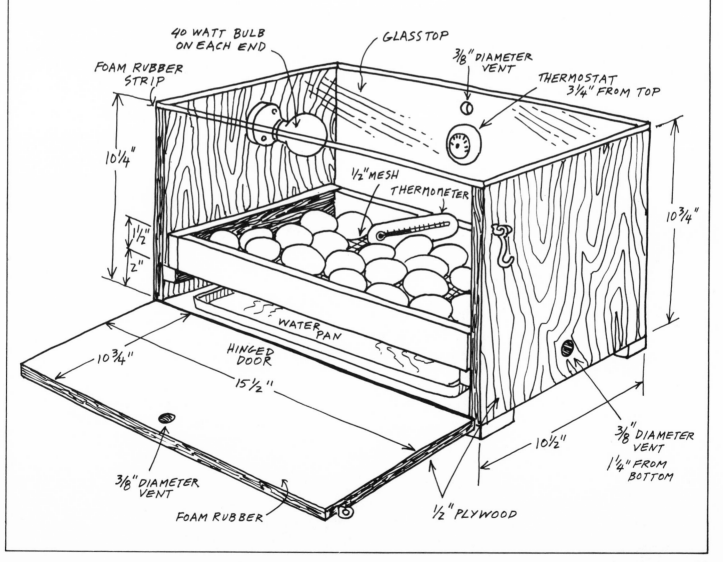

FOAM RUBBER STRIP

40 WATT BULB ON EACH END

GLASS TOP

3/8" DIAMETER VENT

THERMOSTAT 3 1/4" FROM TOP

10 1/4"

1/2"

2"

1/2" MESH

THERMOMETER

10 3/4"

WATER PAN

10 3/4"

HINGED DOOR

15 1/2"

10 1/2"

3/8" DIAMETER VENT

3/8" DIAMETER VENT 1 1/4" FROM BOTTOM

FOAM RUBBER

1/2" PLYWOOD

# Material and Tool Listings
# for Selected Projects

## Sawhorse
*page 13*

| Materials | | Hardware | Tools |
|---|---|---|---|
| amt. | dimensions | | |
| 1 | 2″ × 6″ × 3′ | nails | circular saw (table saw should be |
| 1 | 1″ × 6″ × 10′ | | helpful for the bevelled cuts) |
| 1 | 1″ × 4″ × 10′ | | protractor |
| 1 | 2″ × 4″ × 1½′ | | |

## Workbench
*page 15*

| Materials | | Hardware | Tools |
|---|---|---|---|
| amt. | dimension | | |
| 1 | 2″ × 10″ × 12′ | nails | circular saw |
| 1 | 2″ × 10″ × 6′ | bolts for frame with nuts | |
| 3 | 2″ × 4″ × 10′ | and washers | |
| 2 | 2″ × 4″ × 8′ | | |
| 1 | 4′ × 6′ | tempered masonite ¼″ thick | |

## Potting Bench
*page 18*

| Materials | | Hardware | Tools |
|---|---|---|---|
| amt. | dimension | | |
| 3 | 2″ × 4″ × 10′ | nails | combination square |
| 1 | 2″ × 4″ × 12′ | | circular saw |
| 1 | 2″ × 4″ × 14′ | | |
| 2 | 2″ × 8″ × 8′ | | |

# Potting Bench
*page 18*

| Materials | | Hardware | Tools |
|---|---|---|---|
| amt. | dimension | | |
| 1 | 2″ × 4″ × 10″ | nails | T-bevel |
| 1 | 2″ × 4″ × 8′ | | protractor |
| 1 | 2″ × 6″ × 36½′ | | combination square |
| 1 | 2″ × 8″ × 10′ | | level |
| | | | circular saw |

# Firewood Brace
*page 22*

| Materials | | Hardware | Tools |
|---|---|---|---|
| amt. | dimension | | |
| 1 | 2″ × 6″ × 4½′ | nails | rafter square (not necessary |
| 1 | 1″ × 3″ × 40″ (approx) | | unless you want a perfect 90°) |

# Sawbuck
*page 23*

| Materials | | Hardware | Tools |
|---|---|---|---|
| amt. | dimension | | |
| 2 | 2″ × 8″ × 8′ | carriage bolts with nuts & washers | drill with bit |
| | | nails | T-bevel |

# Fuel Sled
*page 24*

| Materials | | Hardware | Tools |
|---|---|---|---|
| amt. | dimension | | |
| 1 | 4″ × 4″ × 6′ (hardwood) | ring bolt | drill and bits |
| 1 | 2″ × 8″ × 6′ | chain or ½″ rope | |
| | | wood screws | |
| | | lag screws and washers | |

# Tomato Ripening Unit
*pages 40–41*

| Materials | | Hardware | Tools |
|---|---|---|---|
| amt. | dimension | | |
| 3 | 2″ × 4″ × 10′ | nails or wood screws | |
| 1 | 2″ × 4″ × 5′ | brads or staples | staplegun if staples are used |
| 15 | 1″ × 4″ × 12′ | | |
| 6 | 1″ × 4″ × 8′ | | |

60 sq. feet of fiberglass screen

# Picnic Bench
*page 44–5*

| Materials | | Hardware | Tools |
|---|---|---|---|
| amt. | dimension | | |
| 2 | 2″ × 4″ × 10′ | 20 bolts with washers and | drill and bit |
| 2 | 2″ × 4″ × 12′ | wing nuts | circular saw |
| 1 | 2″ × 4″ × 16′ | | protractor |
| 2 | 1″ × 6″ × 12′ | | |
| 1 | 1″ × 6″ × 10′ | galvanized nails | |
| | | wood preservative | |
| | | 2 5″ tee hinges with removeable pin | |

# Lawn Chair
*page 46–47*

| Materials | | Hardware | Tools |
|---|---|---|---|
| amt. | dimension | | |
| 1 | 1″ × 3″ × 12′ | flathead wood screws | T-bevel |
| 1 | 1″ × 3″ × 8′ | | combination square |
| 1 | 1″ × 2″ × 14′ | paint or water seal | |
| 1 | 1″ × 8″ × 12′ | | protractor |
| 1 | 2″ × 2″ × 26½″ | | circular saw |
| 1 | 1″ × 6″ × 23½″ | | |
| 1 | 1″ × 4″ × 4′ | | |

# Mail Box
*page 49*

| Materials | | Hardware | Tools |
|---|---|---|---|
| amt. | dimension | | |
| 1 | 1″ × 18″ rod or pipe | 5d nails | brace (or access to a drill press) |
| 1 | 4″ × 4″ × 5′ | waterproof glue | and 1″ bit |

| Materials | Hardware | Tools |
| amt.  dimension | | |
|---|---|---|
| (pressure treated) | rafter square | |
| 1  4" × 4" × 3' | | circular saw |
| 1  2" × 4" × 1' | | level |
| 1  1" × 10" × 4'5" | | |
| bag of concrete | | |

## Handy Composter
*page 73*

| Materials | Hardware | Tools |
| amt.  dimension | | |
|---|---|---|
| 8  2" × 2" × 10' | 8 screen door hooks | rafter square |
| 96 square feet of 1" mesh | brads | saw |
|    chicken wire | drywall or wood screws | drill and bit |

## Large Sifter
*page 86*

| Materials | Hardware | Tools |
| amt.  dimension | | |
|---|---|---|
| 1  1" × 6" × 8' | nails or drywall screws | combination square |
| 1  2" × 2" × 22" × | 2  3" or ½" bolts with 4 washers | 9/32" bit |
| 2  1" × 6" × 10' |    and 2 nuts | drill |
| | carpenter's glue | saw |
| | wood preservative | |

## Berry Box
*page 95*

| Materials | Hardware | Tools |
| amt.  dimension | | |
|---|---|---|
| 1  1" × 3" × 5' | nails or drywall screws | protrator or combination square |
| 1  1" × 2" × 8' | carpenter's glue | |

## Plant Supports
*pages 102–103*

| Materials | Hardware | Tools |
| amt.  dimension | | |
|---|---|---|
| 3 pcs lath (3/8" × 1" × 4') | | drill & bits |
| 16'  galvanized wire | water sealer | pliers |

# Garden Bench
*page 128*

| *Materials* | | *Hardware* | *Tools* |
|---|---|---|---|
| *amt.* | *dimension* | | |
| 1 | 2″ × 12″ × 8′ | flathead wood screws | hand or circular saw |
| 1 | 2″ × 4″ × 4′ | or | |
| | | galvanized nails | |

waterproof glue

# Folding Bench
*page 130–131*

| *Materials* | | *Hardware* | *Tools* |
|---|---|---|---|
| *amt.* | *dimension* | | |
| 3 | 1″ × 4″ × 10′ | 4 carriage bolts | jig saw |
| 1 | ¾″ × 2″ × 10′ | with | drill |
| 1 | ½″ × 1¼″ × 12′ | 4 nuts and | circular saw |
| 1 | 2″ × 2″ × 14″ | 8 washers | T-bevel |
| | | galvanized nails or wood screws | |

wood scrap for button

# Birdhouse
*page 135*

| *Materials* | | *Hardware* | *Tools* |
|---|---|---|---|
| *amt.* | *dimension* | | |
| 1 | 1″ × 8″ × 8′ | nails or wood screws | drill |
| 1 | ¼″ × 2″ dowel | glue | hole saw or jig saw |
| | | | hand saw or circular saw |

# Hog House
*page 142–143*

| *Materials* | | *Hardware* | *Tools* |
|---|---|---|---|
| *amt.* | *dimension* | | |
| 1 | 2″ × 6″ × 12′ | galvanized nails | circular saw |
| 1 | 2″ × 6″ × 14′ | 2 sets of hinges (either Tee | protractor or T-bevel |
| 2 | 2″ × 3″ × 10′ | or strap) | rafter square |
| 3 | 2″ × 3″ × 12′ | 1 door latch or 1 bolt, | level or plumb bob |
| 5 | 2″ × 3″ × 16′ | 4 washers | |
| 4 | sheets of 3/8″ exterior plywood | | |

# Movable Shed
*page 145–147*

| *Materials* | | *Hardware* | *Tools* |
|---|---|---|---|
| *amt.* | *dimension* | | |
| 3 | 4″ × 4″ × 13′ | galvanized nails | circular saw |
| 2 | 2″ × 6″ × 12′ | framing anchors, metal straps | bevel or protractor |
| 15 | 2″ × 4″ × 8′ | or 3/8″ bolts | level or plumb bob |
| 7 | 2″ × 4″ × 10′ | 3 sets of hinges | |

| Materials | | Hardware | Tools |
|---|---|---|---|
| amt. | dimension | | |
| 8 | 2" × 4" × 12' | 2 door latches, 1 window latch | |
| 7 | 2" × 4" × 14' | 3 folding braces | |
| 4 | 1" × 4" × 10' | | |
| 1 | 1" × 4" × 14' | | |
| 2 | 1" × 6" × 18' | | |
| 4½ | sheets of 3/4" exterior plywood (4' × 8') | | |
| 10½ | sheets of 3/8" exterior plywood (4' × 8') | | |
| 165 | square feet of roofing material (roll roofing) | | |
| tar | | | |
| tar paper | | | |

## Portable Horse Stable
*pages 151–3*

| Materials | | Hardware | Tools |
|---|---|---|---|
| amt. | dimension | | |
| 4 | 4" × 6" × 12' (pressure treated) | galvanized nails roofing nails | protractor level |
| 28 | 2" × 4" × 8' | | circular saw |
| 12 | 2" × 4" × 10' | strap hinges and latch for | |
| 7 | 2" × 4" × 12' | door | |
| 7 | 2" × 4" × 14' | | |
| 4 | 2" × 8" × 12' | | |
| 2 | 1" × 10" × 12' | | |

5 sheets corrugated metal roofing
1 sheet corrugated translucent plastic roofing
8 sheets of ½" exterior plywood

## Corral Gate
*page 154*

| Materials | | Hardware | Tools |
|---|---|---|---|
| amt. | dimension | | |
| 9 | 2" × 6" × 12' | 3/8" machine bolts, nuts and washers | circular saw drill |
| 1 | 2" × 6" × 4' | 2 car spring hinges | |
| 1 | 2" × 6" × 16' | 1 rake tooth | |
| 1 | 1" × 6" × 2' | 1 piece of ¼" × 1" × 20" strap iron | |
| 1 | 2" × 3" × 4½' | 2 screw-in eye bolts | |

## Goat Milking Stand
*page 155*

| Materials | | Hardware | Tools |
|---|---|---|---|
| amt. | dimension | | |
| 3 | 1" × 4" × 10' | galvanized nails | circular saw |
| 2 | 1" × 4" × 12' | hook and eye | jig saw |
| 1 | 1" × 8" × 14' | | |

| Materials | | Hardware | Tools |
|---|---|---|---|
| amt. | dimension | | |
| 1 | 2″ × 3″ × 8′ | | |
| 1 | 1″ × 2″ × 6′ | | |

## Chicken Feeder #1
*page 160*

| Materials | | Hardware | Tools |
|---|---|---|---|
| amt. | dimension | | |
| 1 | 1″ × 12″ × 8′ | galvanized nails | drill |
| 1 | 1″ × 10″ × 12′ | 2) 3/8″ × 2″ carriage bolts | |
| 1 | 1″ × 6″ × 6′ | with nuts & washers | |
| 1 | 1″ × 4″ × 10′ | | |
| 1 | 1″ × 2″ × 16′ | | |
| 1 | ¼″ × 1¼″ × 10′ | | |

## Chicken Feeder #2
*page 161*

| Materials | | Hardware | Tools |
|---|---|---|---|
| amt. | dimension | | |
| 1 | 1″ × 8″ × 8′ | 2) 1¾″ × ¼″ bolts with | drill |
| 1 | 1″ × 4″ × 12′ | washer & wing nuts | router or jig saw |
| 1 | ¼″ × 1¼″ × 6′ | 2) 1¾″ × ¼″ round head | circular saw |
| | | wood screws & washers | |
| | | galvanized nails | |

## Chicken Feeder #3
*page 161*

| Materials | | Hardware | Tools |
|---|---|---|---|
| amt. | dimension | | |
| 1 | 1″ × 6″ × 12′ | galvanized nails | could be done with a hand saw |
| 1 | ¼″ × 1¼″ × 6′ | 1 coil spring | |
| | | 2 eye hooks | |